# $\mathcal{A}$ Children and Prayer
Shared Pilgrimage

# Children and Prayer
## A Shared Pilgrimage

*by*

Betty Shannon Cloyd

UPPER ROOM BOOKS

NASHVILLE

*Children and Prayer: A Shared Pilgrimage*

Art Direction: Michele Wetherbee
Cover Design: Stefan Gutemuth
Photograph: © 1996 Michele Clement
Interior Design: Charles Sutherland
First Printing: February 1997 (5)

Printed in the United States of America

*Library of Congress Cataloging-in-Publication Data*

Cloyd, Betty Shannon.
     Children and prayer: a shared pilgrimage / by Betty Shannon Cloyd.
        p.      cm.
     Includes bibliographical references.
     ISBN 0-8358-0803-3 (pbk.)
      1. Christian education—Home training. 2. Prayer—Christianity.
    3. Children—Religious life. I. Title.
     BV1590.C56   1997
     248.3'2'083—dc20                     96—46093
                                                       CIP

*For my children,*

Mark, Cindy, Tim, and Suzanne
and their spouses Tereese, Jim, Rebecca, Scott,
and for my granddaughter, Maggie, who have all
brought the spirit of God to my life;
and for Tom, my best friend and soul mate
in this pilgrimage of faith.

# CONTENTS

# Preface

⌒

Children have always held a special place in my heart. They have been a vital part of my life as I have worked with them in public schools, in mission schools in Africa and among Native Americans, and in various church settings across the United States. My own four children have had a great part in the fulfillment of my life, as has my granddaughter. In recent years, I have become more and more concerned about the plight of children in our churches, in our communities, in our country, and in our world. They seem to be so hurried, so herded, so hassled. The carefree days of childhood seem to be nonexistent.

Not only have I been concerned about our children's physical lives, but I have an even greater concern for their spiritual lives. The spiritual nature of most children seems to be terribly underdeveloped and often neglected. From this concern, much of my reading and research in the past few years have been on the subject of children and spiritual formation.

When I was participating in the Academy for Spiritual Formation and was assigned a second year project, I chose a subject close to my heart—children and prayer. As a part of that project, I interviewed children of various races and ages about their belief in God and about their prayer life. Most of the children had some church background, but some of them came from homes where the parents did not attend church. As I continued to expand the project, this book came into being.

The words of the children, the ideas they expressed, the light on their faces as we talked about spiritual matters touched me deeply. In this book I have tried especially hard to be true to what I heard the children saying, both in their words and in their body language. I am delighted to share some of these interviews with you throughout the book. Also, the prayers on each chapter's opening page were printed just as the children wrote them. Only illegible words were corrected to make the copy readable.

Although this book is about children and prayer, I do not claim to be an expert in either. My children have taught me just as much as I have taught them, and I often wish that I could have one more chance to parent them. I read once that life is a strange teacher. It gives you the tests first and the answers second. Not that I have all the answers now, but I believe I have some of them. I wish also that when my children were small I had known some of the things that I now know about prayer and the spiritual life. My children and I have been pilgrims praying and learning together and perhaps that was how it should be.

I am grateful to Janice Grana, Robin Pippin, Jan Knight, JoAnn Miller, Sarah Linn, and Karen F. Williams for their belief that this project had the potential to become a book. Their encouragement along the way has been most appreciated.

My thanks too goes to Millie S. Goodson, Marion Parr, and Suzanne Cloyd Hultman for reading the manuscript and for offering their suggestions and ideas. Their help has been invaluable. Finally, I am grateful to my husband, Tom, who helped in many ways to bring this project to completion.

Betty Shannon Cloyd
April 1996

# INTRODUCTION

*C*hildren are a gift from God and, therefore, should be our most precious treasure. Yet when we, as Christian care-givers of children, read about the many atrocities that are happening to children in our world today, of thousands of children dying from hunger and malnutrition each day, thousands more living in poverty, and still thousands more suffering abuse and neglect, we question whether our society and our world value children at all.

In addition to the neglect and abuse of children that confront us daily from our television screens and newspapers, it is apparent that there is another form of poverty impacting children around the world. Although this form is harder to detect and measure, its force is seen in the lives of both affluent and impoverished children. This poverty is spiritual poverty—that void in the child's life of not knowing that he or she is divinely created and infinitely loved by God; that lack of spiritual grounding that gives life meaning and hope.

One factor that contributes to this spiritual poverty is that in recent years we have spent a great deal of time and energy dealing with adult issues. We have been concerned with the inner self, about who we are as individuals, and about how to meet our unmet needs. We have paid a great deal of attention to our own development, to exploring our own potential, and to maximizing our own ego strengths. As important as these are, unfortunately, this self-preoccupation has resulted in the neglect of the child in our midst.

Leonard Sweet in his book *Faithquakes* says that we as a nation have been obsessed in recent years with the "inner child" and "personal growth." He says that it is time for the "outer child," the actual child in our home, our society, and the world to be lauded as well. He continues by saying that it is time now for the child "to be treated as a responsible and highly valued member of society, and of the church."[1]

Another factor that has contributed to this spiritual void is the rushed childhood syndrome. In the last decade, our society has come to view childhood as a time to be hurried through in order to arrive at the often perceived "better stage" of adulthood. Some indications of this hurrying is seen in the adult style clothes and cosmetics that children are permitted to wear, and adult theme television programs and movies that children are allowed to see. As children are rushed at breakneck speed through childhood into adolescence and then on into adulthood, the wondrous days of childhood are often lost and the spiritual nature of the child is frequently neglected.

If we as people of faith, value our children, we will recognize that one of our most significant responsibilities is to help them stay in touch with their spiritual selves. In order for children to be able to do this, they need to be allowed time and space to grow in their understanding of God. We must help them to realize that they have come from God and that the One who created them longs to be in a continual relationship with them. Children need to be aware that God has indeed created them and called them into being (Jeremiah 1:5). A mysterious bond exists between God and the child, and the adults in the child's life have the responsibility to see that that relationship continues to grow. For a person to be spiritually developed he or she needs to have his or her spiritual nature nurtured and nourished. Ultimately children must come to understand that God loves them with an everlasting love not because of what they do, or what they look like, or how they perform, or what they accomplish in life but because God has created them and loves them unconditionally.

For centuries the home was seen as the primary source for nurturing the child in the spiritual life. Learning the scripture, training in the life of prayer and instruction in moral and spiritual values were a vital part of the home life of almost every child. In the last few decades, however, the emphasis changed and the Sunday school and the church have come to be seen as the major source for Christian training with the home taking a secondary role. This factor too has contributed to spiritual poverty. We are now realizing that although Sunday school teachers have done their best, one hour on Sunday is not enough to adequately provide the kind of Christian nurture, guidance and training that our children need. The emphasis must once again be assumed by the home and by the primary adults in the child's life. The Sunday school and the church should, of course, continue to be formative influences in the life of the child, but the major responsibility for training the child in the life of faith must be assumed by the adult(s) in the home. It is time for parents to reclaim that role.

As caregivers one of the ways to do this is to assume the extremely important task of modeling for the child the life of faith. This book is concerned mainly with how the adult can model the life of prayer for children while at the same time, help them grow in their own unique prayer life with God. We may say, "Oh, I can't teach the child how to pray because I don't know how myself." I hope that this book will help you in your own pilgrimage of prayer, even as you are teaching the child to pray. Ideas, resources, illustrations, and examples are given to aid you in both these endeavors.

To help the child learn to pray is not so threatening a task as one might first suppose because, in reality, it is the Holy Spirit who teaches. When we do not know how to pray, the Holy Spirit intercedes for us.

We, as adults, are the gateopeners of this work of the Holy Spirit. When we realize this, we see our task as that of fostering a milieu of hospitality, a place that says "welcome" to the Holy Spirit. In order to facilitate this process, we must create time and space so that this encounter can take place. And we find strength for our task because we realize that we are not in it alone.

It has been said that we are not human beings trying to have a spiritual experience, but we are spiritual beings having a human experience. Prayer is the avenue by which we are enabled to remain in ongoing relationship with the One who has created us as spiritual beings. May God bless you and the child you cherish as you take a pilgrimage of prayer together.

# CHAPTER ONE

## Let the Children Come

Dear God,

Thank you for trees so we can breathe. Thank you for food. thank you for church. amen.

Trent, age 9

*J*esus had a great love for children. He commented that their simple trust and faith enabled them to see clearly the things of the spirit. One of the most moving stories from the Gospels tells us of the loving relationship that Jesus had with children. Mark recounts it in this way:

> People were bringing little children to him in order that he might touch them; and the disciples spoke sternly to them. But when Jesus saw this, he was indignant and said to them, 'Let the little children come to me; do not stop them; for it is to such as these that the kingdom of God belongs. Truly I tell you, whoever does not receive the kingdom of God as a little child will never enter it.' And he took them up in his arms, laid his hands on them, and blessed them.
>
> Mark 10:13-16

Jesus also cited children as an example of what it meant to be the ideal member of the realm of God. "Truly, I tell you, unless you become like children," he tells us, "you will never enter the kingdom of heaven" (Matthew 18:2).

Some persons believe that since children have so recently come from God, they are closer to God than those of us who have lived a longer time. We adults have accumulated many layers of baggage along the way; baggage which sometimes keeps us from being totally trusting and honest with God. My friend Nancy who works closely with children has written:

There is something so moving about the purity and innocence of childhood. Children are closer to God for they haven't yet acquired all the trappings of religion—administrative procedures, theological doctrine, political power plays. They know only of trusting, believing, and freely giving their unconditional love! They touch us deeply, for they remind us of qualities lost and worth recapturing. Truly we know what Jesus meant when he said, "Whoever does not receive the kingdom of God as a little child will never enter it."[1]

I believe Nancy is right when she says that Jesus saw in children some of the qualities which we have lost and wish we could regain. For instance, the candor that children display is so refreshing. Sometimes their honesty can be embarrassing but it is, nonetheless, refreshing! They have no hidden agendas, no political power plays. They speak the truth as they see it—and they speak from the heart.

Have you ever observed the curiosity of a child—the endless questions they ask, especially questions about God?—"Who made God?" "Where does God live?" "What does God look like?" They are intrigued with spiritual matters and have an insatiable desire to learn all they can from life. And if they don't know the answers, they are not afraid to ask because to find the answers to life's questions is their most important quest. I think Jesus must have valued the trustfulness and sense of dependence that children have when crises come. Children do not pretend to be self-sufficient as we do, and they are quick to admit their need for help. In one interview I had, Mollie, age five, said, "God is good to us and is always by our side." She believed that God was with her when she had a great need. Rachel, also five, when asked about God said, "God is very special. He is all around you even though you don't know it. God protects you and heals you too when you are sick." Another quality we see in children and one which must have been embraced by Jesus is their sense of wonder and awe. My granddaughter, Maggie, has taught me anew what it means to have a sense of wonder and what it means to have the joy of a playful spirit. To give myself in reckless abandon to a game of tag or of hide and seek does much for my spirit. To view a beautiful butterfly in flight and to remember that God has created all things, renews my faith. To marvel at a sunset or the vastness of the ocean with a child and to observe a sense of awe and wonder is re-creating. Children are very quick to recognize that there is a Higher Being who has created the world and is still in control of it. In talking with Robert, nine years old, I asked him if he could remember the first time he felt God's presence in his life. He thought a minute and answered, "Yes, I remember. I saw this big yellow sun, and it reminded me of God. At first I thought it was God, but then I saw it was the sun that God had made, and that reminded me of Him." Children are quick to give God credit for all of creation.

Children seem to have an uncanny sense of their connectedness with God. The story of two young children illustrates this sense of their belonging to God. When the older child was three years old, a newborn sister was brought home from the hospital. The older child kept insisting that his mother allow him to be alone for awhile with his new baby sister. At first the mother hesitated, not knowing the child's intentions. But the older child persisted, and finally the mother gave in. She stood outside the door where the child could not see her, but where she could see and hear everything that went on in the room. The older child walked slowly to the crib, leaned carefully over it, and in a hushed voice said to the baby, "Tell me about God. I think I'm beginning to forget."[2] Perhaps there is much that we have forgotten about God and the spiritual life that we can re-learn from children. We know from the gospel stories that Jesus did, indeed, love children. He placed their status above that of the religious leaders, above the politically powerful, and above the socially elite of his day. And as is related in the gospel story, he gives us the solemn admonition that unless  we receive the kingdom of  God, the realm of  God, as a little child, we will never enter it. "Let the little children come to me," he said, "for it is to such as these that the kingdom of God belongs."

Jesus' love for children and the trust and faith that he placed in them, models for us what our relationship with children should be. Because of their specialness to Jesus, they should be recognized as our most valued treasure as well. As such, we as Christian caregivers, must realize that one of our most important tasks in life is to spend time with children, to mentor and guide them, and to help them keep in touch with the One who has called them into being. For it is only in knowing to whom they belong that they know who they are. Their identity is found in God.

As we think about children and their spiritual growth, we need to review some of the studies that have been done involving the spirituality of children. Robert Coles, a psychiatrist and professor, has for many years conducted studies with children. In his book *The Spiritual Life of Children* he says, this study has "helped me see children as seekers, as young pilgrims well aware that life is a finite journey and as anxious to make sense of it as those of us who are farther along in the time allotted us."[3]

In his extensive work, Dr. Coles interviewed children about their understanding of God. He visited with children who were Christian, Moslem, Jewish, and with children who had no religious background. He interviewed children from various cultures: American, Irish, Tunisian, Israeli, American Indian, and others. He also studied children from every social strata in life: wealthy children, children from Appalachia, poor children, children from the inner city. His findings were significant.

Regardless of their nationality, their social strata, or whether they were reared in a religious environment, children everywhere, he concluded, have a deep awareness of God and the spiritual life. Truly, as the old adage goes, children and God speak the same language.[4]

Marlene Halpin, a Dominican Sister, has also done extensive studies regarding children and prayer. She too has concluded that there is a deep spiritual nature in children which must be nurtured and nourished. Prayer and our relationship with God is crucial to this effort.[5]

In the ministry in which my husband, Tom, and I have been involved, we have found that children have a spirituality regardless of where and under what circumstances they were born. Both in Zaire, Africa, and on the Navajo Reservation, we saw a spirituality among children that touched our hearts. In churches across the United States, we have been grateful for the presence of children and have been enriched by their understanding of God.

In one of the churches where we were in ministry, I remember a young mother recounting this story. One day, her little girl who was about four years old at the time, came running into the house after walking a short distance to the mailbox.

Her eyes were bright and her face flushed. She was visibly excited as she exclaimed, "God did it, God did it, Mama!"

"Did what?" her mother inquired.

"God spoke to me," Jennifer declared. "I had been asking God to speak to me, and on the way to the mailbox today, God did it!" With complete lack of embarrassment and with ultimate trust in a faithful God, she related this story to her mother. She had expected God to answer her prayer and God did. It was as simple as that.

During the Second World War, my father was drafted even though he was much older than most of the other draftees. My mother was left with four children and very meager funds. Each year while my father was away, we planted a large garden, partly because it was the patriotic thing to do, but primarily because we desperately needed the vegetables to supplement our resources.

One day, as we sat down to our noon meal, my mother had a very serious look on her face. "Children," she said, "our garden is very dry. If it doesn't rain soon, we will lose all of our vegetables. If that happens, we will not have food to eat now nor any to can for the winter months. Let's pray now before we eat and tell God our need." We bowed our heads and my mother prayed a simple prayer, telling God how desperately we needed rain and ending by thanking God for hearing and answering our prayer.

Just as we finished our meal, my brother, who was the youngest child in the family, disappeared from the table. In a few minutes he was back, carrying with him his truck, his army men and other toys he had been playing with in the yard. My mother asked him what he was doing. "Well," he said, "I went to get my toys in before it starts to rain."

Children are like that. They have a formula and it is simple: we have a need, we present it to God, God hears our prayers and God answers. In childlike faith, they present their needs to God trusting in a God who is able and willing to answer.

Jesus said so long ago, "Let the children come, because it is to such as these that the kingdom of God belongs." Whether we are a parent, grandparent, or another significant adult in the child's life, rearing children is a tremendous challenge and a sacred opportunity. With all the brokenness and pain that is present in a world alien to the things of the Spirit, our responsibility is to provide a place of hospitality, a place where the Holy Spirit is welcomed in our lives and in the lives of our children. Through a life of prayer we can become gateopeners, allowing the winds of the Spirit to enter.

# CHAPTER TWO

## To Such as These

Dear God,

We thank you for food we eat,
the clothes we wear, and the roof
that we live under. We pray for
the people that have no home
and that they will find a home.
And we pray for all the people in
the hospital that they get well.

Erin, age 8

*A*s we are considering helping children grow in their experience of prayer, we must have an understanding of what prayer is. There are, of course, many definitions.

1. "The most important thing in prayer is never what we say or ask for, but our attitude towards God." Evelyn Underhill[1]
2. "All true prayer is person-to-Person communion and encounter with God." Mack B. Stokes[2]
3. "Prayer is certainly the grand means of drawing near to God." John Wesley[3]
4. "True, whole prayer is nothing but love." Saint Augustine[4]
5. "Prayer is the central avenue God uses to transform us." Richard Foster[5]
6. "Prayer is an encounter and a relationship [with God]." Archbishop Anthony Bloom[6]

These definitions work well for adults who live and work with children. We understand the words and their implications for us. But for children, we need definitions that they can grasp and make their own. One definition of prayer that I have found to be helpful for children is this: Prayer is using our own words to talk with and listen to God at any time, at any place, and about any thing.

The definition and understanding of prayer that children form in their early years will be a guiding force for them in their life-long spiritual journey. Laying a solid foundation is important because children need to have a positive concept of the true meaning of prayer. Misconceptions are hard to unlearn.

What we want to do most of all is to help children find their own special way of expressing their feelings to God. C. S. Lewis has said that in prayer we "lay before [God] what is in us, not what ought to be in us."[7] This is an important concept for all of us to learn. We can tell God everything that is in our hearts. Children need to understand that it is all right to express all of their feelings to God, and they need to be assured that God hears and understands.

We must avoid forcing our way of praying upon children. Children should be allowed to pray in their own words and in their own way. Their spontaneity and sincerity are entirely adequate for an ongoing relationship with a loving God.


## ASSUMPTIONS ABOUT CHILDREN'S SPIRITUAL DEVELOPMENT

As we think about children and prayer, and about their spiritual growth, we must explore some assumptions about their religious development. In addition to Robert Coles' and Marlene Halpin's research, Sofia Cavalletti has done outstanding studies on the religious potential of children. In her book *The Religious Potential of the Child*, which chronicles her findings, she speaks of several assumptions that she has drawn with regard to the religious development of children. The first of these, she says, is that we assume that children experience God. If we did not have this assumption, there would not be a possibility of the child having an ongoing, open communication and relationship with God. The child may not be able to articulate the experience well or might, for fear of ridicule, hesitate to speak of it. In some cases a child may not refer to his or her experience without encouragement, but nonetheless, the assumption is that the child is capable of and does have valid experiences of God.

These experiences are spontaneous and do not come at the prompting of an adult. They are authentic experiences of God as many other studies bear out. Such studies show the child is capable of having religious experiences typical of and just as valid as those of adolescents and adults. These experiences are not imitations of the experiences of others but are authentic in themselves and are deeply significant to the child.

Second, Cavalletti says we assume "that the child's religious potential is a global experience in two ways." By global she means that this religious potential touches the child's total being and is not just some isolated part of the child's development. Additionally, by global, she says that the religious potential of the child is natural, "so it is essential to what defines being human regardless of where the child is born on the globe." This is verified by Robert Coles and others who have done extensive study on the subject.

Third, Cavalletti says, we assume that "human beings are not fully developed unless their religious potential is stimulated and growing." Prayer is certainly a major way that helps this growth to take place. Spiritual growth is intrinsic to human health, wholeness, and well-being. In our society, we are just beginning to understand this concept. For instance, in many emergency rooms now, there is a chaplain on call just as there is a physician, a social worker, and a psychiatrist. It is becoming more and more recognized that the spiritual part of the human being needs attention, just as the physical body needs attention.

A fourth assumption Cavalletti proposes is that the religious language of the Judeo-Christian tradition "is a language that is very powerful as an agent to describe, evoke, and express" the child's experience of God. Further, in the Judeo-Christian tradition, we have great models of prayer that can guide and enhance the child's prayer life. The Bible gives us many powerful models of prayer, and our Christian tradition gives us the words that enable us to pray.[8]

To Cavalletti's assumptions, I would like to add two of my own. The first is I believe that what the child comes to believe about God greatly affects the way the child will pray to God. That is, if the child sees God as a harsh and cruel deity, the child will pray in a different way than if God is seen as a benevolent, loving parent. I remember cringing once at a church where I was working when I overheard a childcare worker saying to a group of three year olds, "God and Jesus won't like you if you do that." I was fearful that this statement, or others similar to it, would give the children a totally erroneous concept of God.

Nothing should ever be said or done to the child that would cause the child to believe that God's love would be removed from her or him. Rather, the fact of God's unconditional love should be proclaimed at all times in all our encounters with children. In interviewing one young boy, age seven, I asked him what he thought God was like. He did not answer. Then I asked what God does for us. His eyes got very wide and he replied, "He'll strap you." I replied, "You know, don't you, that God loves you very much?" He brightened then and said, "Yes, I know, God is love." I was very troubled by his first comment.

If children come to believe that God is watching their every move and is ready to pounce on them for any wrong doing, they will be conditioned in their prayers by this concept. The "God will get you" theory must never be taught to children. Some years ago when my children were small, we were living in the Southwest. A friend of ours gave us a huge *Ojo de Dios* (Eye of God) to hang on our wall. It was the largest one I had ever seen, measuring perhaps three feet tall and three feet wide. Since the color scheme used in the *ojo* was compatible with the colors in my oldest son's room, I hung it there over his bed. It remained there for several days without much being said about it. Finally one day, Mark came to me and said, "Mom, please take that *ojo* out of my room. I don't want God seeing everything that I do." I realized that I had some work to do with his concept of God. He needed to understand that God is more like a tender shepherd who cares for us than a God who is out to get us for any little infraction of the rules. Although God knows what we do, God loves us anyway.

Likewise, if children see God as a giant Santa Claus in the sky, they will pray a certain way. Children will come to believe that if they want anything at all, they just have to ask the eternal Santa Claus and it will be granted. This concept of God greatly limits the prayer power of the child. Just as loving parents have to say "no" to their children's requests sometimes, God must say no to us as well. Sometimes too for our own good, God has to say "wait a while," delaying whatever we are praying for. In this day of instant gratification, this is a difficult concept for adults to comprehend and is certainly harder for children to grasp.

On the other hand, if God is seen as weak and ineffective, a "don't care" God who doesn't hear or care about us, children will pray in a half-hearted way. There will be no fervor or expectation in their prayers because this kind of God doesn't help us much anyway. Jediah, age eight, said in the interview I had with him, "God helps us. When bad things happen or someone dies or gets in trouble, God is there." He believed in a God who was strong and effective.

We must be careful what we teach about God because unlearning is hard to do. Especially is this true for the child if what was learned in error was learned from a trusted and well-loved adult. Sometimes in the unlearning, serious doubts about who God is and what God can do arise. We want to avoid this if at all possible. I believe, then, that in our teaching and training of children, how we interpret God to them is crucial. What we teach about God is all important to the child's prayer life for the present time and for the rest of her or his life. In *The Good Shepherd and the Child*, Sofia Cavalletti says that we must give children chances to "fall in love with God."[9] This is how we want them to view God; that God is love and that God loves them unconditionally.

The second assumption I would like to propose about the religious development of children is that some children are by nature more contemplative than others. Some children, from the time they are born, are more reflective and deeper in their thinking.[10] Their spirits are more in rhythm with the life of the Spirit of God.

We know so much more now about personality types than we did several years ago. And we are increasingly aware that the personality type with which we are born greatly affects our spirituality. Some of us tend to be extroverted, others more introverted. Some of us are intuitive, others more analytical. Some children are extremely observant of their surroundings, others not. Some are stirred by things of beauty, others by activity.

We need to be aware of this information as we engage children in the things of the spirit. Not all children will be motivated or touched by what we attempt with them. We must observe and learn what best suits each child. If music speaks best, use music. If quietness speaks to the child, use quiet times. With time, we will learn the personality of each child and will become more aware of which methods help the child to *"fall in love"* with God.

The following statements provide several positive and negative concepts about God. Of course, we want to emphasize the positive concepts with children and avoid the negative.

**Positive Concepts about God**

1. God is love and God is good.
2. God called us into being, loves us very much, and knows what is best for us.
3. God has many characteristics: Creator, Comforter, Loving Parent, Friend.
4. God is active in our world.
5. God will always listen and understand.
6. God has given us freedom to make decisions and helps us in our choices.
7. God may not like some of the things we do but loves us anyway.
8. God is infinite (everlasting).
9. God is a spirit (understanding of this concept will come with time).

**Negative Concepts about God**

1. God is a harsh God.
2. God is unfair.
3. God is "out to get us." (God is a snoop, watching our every move.)
4. God causes bad things to happen to us and to others.
5. God always gives us what we ask.

## CHILDREN LEARN TO PRAY BEST BY OUR MODELING

We know that children learn in many ways: they learn by observation, by participation, by repetition, and by stimulation. These valid ways of learning can be employed in teaching the child to pray. However, I believe that the best way for the child to learn to pray is by our own modeling the life of prayer.

In speaking with adults about their prayer life and asking them how they learned to pray, almost without exception, they named some loved one whom they observed in prayer. One man spoke of his grandfather who prayed with his open Bible on his knees; one spoke of hearing his father in prayer after the family had gone to bed in the evening. Another spoke of the faith of her mother and of hearing her mother pray beautiful faith-filled prayers.

In speaking with children, I heard them quickly identify persons who had modeled prayer for them. When I asked them who had taught them how to pray, they named significant adults whom they had observed in prayer. Jamie, age eleven, mentioned her minister and her grandfather, Grace named her mother, and John, his father. They all felt that by the example and instructions from significant adults, they, themselves, had learned how to pray.

We know too that children learn by unspoken and unnamed agendas. They learn by the ambiance of feelings around them and are like magnets drawing to themselves all the vibes, good and bad, that are present where they are. The life we live speaks a great deal to children: how we go about our daily chores, how we view the world, how we deal with others, what occupies our thoughts and our time. Sometimes what we do and who we are truly speak louder than the words we use. If we learn to practice the presence of God in all that we do and live so as to reflect the spirit of God, these unspoken actions speak volumes to children. When I asked Katie, twelve, who was closer to God than anyone she knew, she mentioned a man in her church who had befriended her brother. Her mother is a single parent and this man had done many acts of kindness for her brother. His Christ-like spirit made her feel the presence of God. Several of the children that I interviewed from the inner city said that Martin Luther King, Jr. was closer to God than anyone they knew.

The life that we model for our children is all important. It says to them that we believe what we say about prayer and the life of the spirit and that the way of prayer is our chosen way of life.

Rachel Carson has a wonderful quote which says: "If a child is to keep alive his [or her] inborn sense of wonder . . . he [or she] needs the companionship of at least one adult who can share it, rediscovering with him [or her] the joy, excitement, and mystery of the world we live in."[11]

I believe that the same is true of the spiritual lives of children: "If the child is to keep alive his or her inborn sense of the [Eternal], he or she needs the companionship of at least one adult who can share it . . ."

# CHAPTER THREE

# *Ages and Stages*

Dear God,

Forgive me for all of my sins. I know when I probably die I will pray to the Lord so my God will take me to heaven. Thank you for saving this world from all of their sins and I know you will always watch over us. No matter if we bad or sweet you will always love us. Aman.

Contina, 4th grade

Dear God,

Thank you for everything I have. Please make my cat better because my mom hit him with the car last night. I 'm glad he doesn't have any broken bones. AMEN.

Blake, age 9

*W*hat is it that determines how and when a child prays? Does the age of the child make a difference? Does the developmental stage of the child determine how the child prays? Does the religious background and training of the child shape the child's prayer life? As one can easily see, these questions could have many answers as the issues involved are so complex.

As we consider the spiritual development of the child, especially as it is related to the child's prayer life, we should note what prominent researchers in child development have said about the stages of development. We cannot look at the spiritual development of the child and totally ignore all other areas of development in childhood. For the child to be a whole and healthy human being, all of the areas of development must be given sufficient attention. Therefore, let us look at some brief descriptions of the theories of development proposed by important child developmentalists.

Jean Piaget, a Swiss psychologist, founded the structural-developmental school of thought and his work has greatly affected the research on child development for several decades. Many authorities in the field have based their work on that of Piaget, using the theories that he developed.

The structural-development theorists propose the following theories about the structures or stages of childhood.

1. The stages are universal. (The same stages in the same order are applicable to every person in every culture.)
2. The stages are sequential. (They follow a set order or pattern.)
3. The stages are invariant. (They build on one another, which means that no stage can be skipped or left out.)
4. The stages are hierarchical. (They go from one step of complexity to another.)[1]

## COGNITIVE DEVELOPMENT

Piaget's stages of cognitive development are helpful to those who are working with the spiritual development of children.

- Stage one—sensorimotor period which is from birth to two years of age;
- Stage two—preoperational period which is from two to seven years of age;
- Stage three—concrete operational period; ages seven to eleven years of age;
- Stage four—formal operational period, ages eleven to adulthood.[2]

## MORAL DEVELOPMENT

Following Piaget's work in cognitive development and using some of his theories, Lawrence Kohlberg has done in-depth study in the area of moral development. He has determined that there are six sequential patterns or stages by which individuals solve moral dilemmas.

- Stage one (ages 3–7) — punishment and obedience orientation: the consequence of the action determines whether it is good or bad regardless of the human meaning or value of these consequences.

- Stage two (8–11) — instrumental relativist orientation: right action is that which satisfies one's own need and sometimes the need of another.

- Stage three (12–17) — interpersonal concordance or "good boy-nice girl" orientation: good behavior is seen as that which helps or pleases others and is approved by them.

- Stage four (18–25) — "law and order" orientation: the focus is on authority, fixed rules, and the maintenance of the social order.

- Stage five (age 25 and older) — social-contract legalistic orientation: the right action would be determined by individual rights and by the standards agreed upon by the whole society.

- Stage six (no age given because so few attain this level) — universal ethical-principle orientation: the right action is determined by the conscience, using high ethical principles that have been chosen by the individual. The principles would be abstract (like the Golden Rule) and would incorporate concepts of human dignity, justice, and the like.[3]

## EMOTIONAL DEVELOPMENT

Erik Erikson's work in psychosocial development has helped us know a great deal about the emotional development of children. His work has also had a great impact on religious educational theory and practice. Erikson feels that the healthy personality also moves through a series of stages, and from his research, he has identified eight distinct stages.

- Stage one — Trust vs. mistrust (the first year of the child's life);

- Stage two—Autonomy vs. shame (ages two through three);
- Stage three—Initiative vs. guilt (generally ages two through four);
- Stage four—Crisis of industry vs. inferiority (usually the school years prior to adolescence);
- Stage five—Identity vs. identity confusion (adolescent);
- Stage six—Intimacy vs. isolation (young adulthood);
- Stage seven—Generativity vs. absorbed with self (adulthood);
- Stage eight—Integrity vs. despair (old age).[4]

## FAITH DEVELOPMENT

James Fowler's study in the area of faith development has concluded that there are six stages in faith development. He views these stages as predictable and irreversible and believes that they advance from one stage of complexity to another over a lifetime. We move through these stages at our own pace and may even get "stuck" in a stage of faith, never advancing any further. Fowler identifies the stages of faith as these:

- Stage one—intuitive-projective faith (ages two-seven): the child is not capable of logical thinking and uses intuition to try to understand God.
- Stage two—mythic-literal faith (ages seven to eleven): children are literal minded and understand faith through the stories, beliefs, and practices of their faith community;
- Stage three—synthetic-conventional faith (ages twelve to eighteen): a person takes the faith of the family or peer group;
- Stage four—individuative-reflective faith (ages eighteen to thirty): persons begin to have their own individual thoughts

about faith and have the ability to express their beliefs; persons are beginning to take responsibility for their commitments;

- Stage five—conjunctive faith: persons begin to see that things are not always black and white, and faith, during this stage, does not provide all the answers;
- Stage six—universalizing faith: (Very few persons reach this stage of faith.) persons live their faith and everything they do is living out of their religious faith and convictions.[5]

Theories of Christian education over the last decades have drawn heavily on the psychological approach to child development. They have included the above-named theories of structural-developmentalism with regard to faith development, believing that the stages are sequential, invariant and hierarchical. As we think about this, it causes us to wonder. Is the Holy Spirit, this mysterious *ruah* of God (breath of God), confined to certain stages? Can the Holy Spirit break into the life of the child regardless of the age or the stage of development of the child?

The stories of faith found in the New Testament and the dynamic narrative of our Christian heritage over the years, tell us that the Holy Spirit is not bound by our human constraints. Nor is the Spirit of God limited by our frailties or summoned by our goodness or by our maturity. The wind blows where it wills, and we hear the sound of it, but do not know from where it comes or where it goes. Indeed, if we value Robert Coles' work and the teachings of Sofia Cavalletti and others, we believe that the inbreaking of the Spirit is not predictable and does not work in stage sequence. A child might have just as valuable an experience of God as someone who is at an advanced developmental stage or further along in years.

However, before we disregard the theories identified by the developmentalists as not applicable to the spiritual development of the child, we must acknowledge that they do, in fact, provide us with helpful insights in identifying and determining certain components of the spiritual process. For instance, we do know from studying the above-mentioned works that there are certain religious concepts that are more easily grasped by the child at one stage than at another. We also know that there are certain religious concepts that the child will cling to at a certain stage, only to give them up when he or she arrives at another stage. Let's look at some of these insights that guide us as we work with the spirituality of the child, particularly the insights that might help us as we guide children in their life of prayer.

Children up to the age of eight view God by simple anthropomorphism; that is, they view God as a human person. From age eight to twelve, God is still seen as human, but different from all other humans.[6] Sometimes the child views God as bigger and stronger and more powerful than other humans. In fact, many children view God as something of a superman. [7] Renzo Vianello conducted a study in 1980 that shows that children ages six to seven, picture God as a giant, a magician, or an invisible man. After the age of eight, the child begins to have an increased understanding of the spiritual nature of God. They might even hesitate to describe God because they do not fully understand the awesome spiritual nature of God.

The majority of children do not understand the concept of God as a spirit until they are teenagers.[8] The responses of children in my interviews verify this fact. Derrick, age five, said that God has a beard. Rachel, age five, said the same, but she added that God has a mustache as well. Kate, age five, said that God is a nice person who lives in the sky, and God has brown hair, green eyes, and wears shorts. When I asked one little boy how he would describe God, he pointed upward and said, "He's the man upstairs." Paige, age seven, said that God has a beard which is blackish brown, and he wears a white and blue robe. Grace, age nine, said that God is very big and nice and that he talks very loud.

Several of the twelve-year-old children I interviewed, however, seem to be moving from simple anthropomorphism to realizing that God has a spiritual nature. John, age twelve, said that he pictured God as a king with a beard and with a mist all around him; but added as an afterthought, that he knew that God wasn't really a person like us. Katie, age twelve, said that she pictured God with a shiny robe but added that she could not describe God's face because God is a spirit. When I asked Ellie, age twelve, if she could describe God, she smiled and said, "Oh, I couldn't do that because God is a Spirit. I guess I could say though, that God is like a rock or like the *alpha* and *omega* or a burning bush."

For children, understanding the spiritual nature of God is a process, and their ability to understand this seems to relate directly to their age and developmental stage.

Only Allison, age three, gave a different description of God. She said that if she were drawing God, she would make a "whole lot of circles on the page and color the whole thing pink, like clouds." Could it be that Allison already understands something of the spiritual nature of God at age three? Could she already perceive that God is not something that can be drawn in human form but can only be described in the abstract? Some studies show that preschoolers perceive God as invisible. (Perhaps this is what Allison was trying to describe.)

Another concept that has come to us from the developmentalists is that of egocentrism in children. That is, they view one's self as the center, object, and norm of all experience. Sometimes children, as Piaget has shown in his studies, have magical thinking in which they believe that their internal thoughts produce external results. That is to say, they believe that thinking certain thoughts result in outward consequences. Piaget says that this is due to egocentric thinking in the child.

The concept of egocentrism in children must be recognized and understood, especially if something tragic happens in the child's life. For example, if a death occurs in the family, the causes of the death should be talked through thoroughly with the child. Perhaps the child, in some fleeting instant—or not so fleeting instant—might have wished that someone would die. If that person should die, the child, through their egocentric or magical thinking, might come to believe that she or he caused the death. Egocentrism applies to divorce as well. If divorce occurs, and the child has had bad thoughts about a parent, she or he might believe that her or his internal thoughts have caused the external consequence. Situations like these should be talked through thoroughly with the child so that the child will understand that what has happened is not his or her fault.

In praying with a child, adults should remember that egocentrism and magical thinking are definitely a part of early childhood and should be expected. We as adults should help children know that neither their words nor their thoughts cause a thing to happen. Prayer is not a magical incantation and should never be viewed as such. Certainly, we know that God hears the words that we speak and knows our thoughts, but God is the author of life and God knows what is best for each one of us. It is God who brings answers to our prayers. It is not the child's words or thoughts. This is a concept that should be explored with children as we work with them in their life of prayer.

It is natural also for children, in their prayer time, to be concerned with "me, my, and mine." This is the world that children know best. Eventually they will be nudged out of their self-centered prayers toward a more mature way of praying. As parents, teachers, and other significant persons in their lives model a more altruistic way of praying, children will also begin to pray in a broader, more inclusive way.

Sigmund Freud believed that the view a person had of God is similar to the concept that the person held of his or her father. Carl Jung, on the other hand, believed that a person's view of God was more like the one held of one's mother.[9] Later studies have shown that children's image of God is more like the father than the mother for both boys and girls.[10] We must be aware, then, as we work with children in the area of prayer and spirituality, that each child's view of God be equated with the most loving, protective, nurturing parent that the child knows. Through

God's grace, even if the child does not have a loving parent, another nurturing adult may provide this image. The children I interviewed spoke of their fathers, their mothers, their aunts, and their pastors as being like God.

Ronald Goldman has helped us see that it is difficult for a child who has not experienced unconditional love at home or in some other significant place to accept the idea that God loves them without reservation.[11] This is why it is so important for the child to know, and to have reinforced in as many ways as possible, that God's love is unconditional.

Studies have shown that the concept of a God who is loving, caring, and forgiving is directly related to positive relationships with parents. As parents, we must heed this knowledge and exemplify to our children unconditional love. This will help them in turn to have a healthy understanding of God's love for them. They should come to know that there is nothing that they can think, do, or say that would cause God to remove God's love from them.

Another insight from the developmental theorists that can help us as we work with the spirituality of children is the issue of justice. Children believe that the punishment should fit the crime, and they place great emphasis on what is fair. How many times, as you have observed children playing a game, have you heard them say, "But that's not fair!" Fairness is very important to them. It is hard, therefore, for them to grasp the belief that God's grace, or God's unconditional love, is available to someone who has done something wrong. Delia Halverson defines God's grace as "I love you anyway."[12] I believe that this is a wonderful way to explain God's grace to children.

Children know when they have hurt someone or said something unkind and should be encouraged to make amends whenever possible. However, they should come to know that although God may not like what they do, God still loves them.

Another concept brought to us by the structural-developmentalists is that children are literal in their interpretation of the world around them. They interpret Bible stories literally and

often, because of their limited ability to think abstractly or logi-
cally, they misunderstand what is being said. They are trying to
make as much sense as possible out of what is being told them but
in the early childhood years, they are not capable of complex,
abstract thinking.

Many examples can be given of this type of thinking. I'm sure
all of us have heard of the child who, when praying the Lord's
prayer, prayed, "Our father who art in heaven, Harold be thy
name." Or of the child who after studying the story of Moses in
Sunday school, goes home and tells his or her own elaborate version of the story. Often it does not have any resemblance to the
original one from the Bible!

Recently my granddaughter, Maggie, age six, was riding with
me as we passed one of our favorite stores. I noticed that they
were doing some renovation on the store and said, "Oh, look, they
are adding a floor to the store." Maggie thought a minute and then
said with a tone in her voice that meant — you ought to know better than that. "Why Shug," (her pet name for me) she said, "that
store has always had a floor. If it hadn't had one, we would have
been walking on dirt."

Recently, as I was telling the story of Paul's experience on the
road to Damascus, a large group of children were gathered
around me. I said, "We don't know whether Paul was riding a
horse and fell to the ground or whether he was walking and fell to
the ground when the light from heaven came upon him." Parker,
age five, raised his hand and said, "I know exactly what happened. He wasn't on a horse. He was walking and just fell to the
ground. I saw the whole thing on a video." We must be very careful about what we say to children and about what they see and
hear, because they take everything very literally.

Knowing this characteristic of children helps us as we teach,
interpret, and guide them. It should help us to more effectively
present religious truths in such a way that the child may both
understand and accept them.

It is interesting to see how children respond when they are

asked, "When do you feel closest to God?" In G. Klingberg's study, he found that children usually say that they feel closest to God in difficult situations. This might be when they are sick or when they are lonely or when they are afraid. Very few said that they felt close to God during a happy event.[13] In the interviews I did this was certainly the case with very few exceptions. Paty and Jessica both said they felt God was the closest to them when their grandfathers died. William said he felt God was very close to him when he was running in a cross-country race and needed strength. Derrick, age five, said he felt God was closest to him when he got hurt. John, age twelve, said he felt God's presence when his parents got a divorce and he was feeling sad.

In contrast to these answers, Rachel, age five, said she felt God was closest to her on her birthday when she was having a good time with her friends and family. Katie, age twelve, said she felt God closest to her when she was at a church camp and the leader was telling a story that made her feel God's presence. The majority of those interviewed, however, said they felt closest to God in times of trouble or sadness or difficulty or fear.

As we work with children, we should take every opportunity to acknowledge God's presence, both in the good times and the bad. In the morning, as we awaken our children, we can affirm God's presence by quoting a verse of scripture such as, "This is the day that the LORD has made; let us rejoice and be glad in it" (Psalm 118:24). Or "Make a joyful noise to the Lord, all the earth. Worship the LORD with gladness; come into his presence with singing" (Psalm 100: 1-2). We can also sing songs that relate our faith in God and our confidence in God's watchful care of us during the day. Janice Grana, the world editor and publisher of the Upper Room, says that as she awakened her two children every morning, she sang to them the song, "Ev'ry morning seems to say, 'There's something happy on the way, and God sends love to you!' "[14]

In this age of uncertainty, violence, and brokenness in the world in which we live, it is vitally important that we relate to our children not only our love, but God's great and unconditional love as well. Our communities, our schools, and our neighborhoods are frightening places for many of our children, and we need to instill in them the knowledge that God is with them and for them, regardless of life's circumstances.

These are, in part, some of the helpful concepts that may be learned from the structural-developmentalists. While they are useful and relevant, they do not in any way place limits on God's activity. To conclude that children must be at a certain developmental stage before they can have an authentic and valid experience of God, limits the power and purpose of God. How the child prays, the words he or she uses and the thoughts expressed, certainly are an indication of the age and stage of the child. But being able to pray and having the capacity to have a valid relationship with God is not limited to a certain age or stage. Just as surely as God's transforming power works in the lives of adults, even so, God works in the lives of children, wherever, whenever, and however God chooses.

# CHAPTER FOUR

## The Wind Blows Where It Will

Dear God in heven,

Look over my family and tack care of them. Thank you for food I eat. Thank you for every thing you give me. Forgive me for everything I did wrong. Thank you for your child. Amen.

Rebecca, age 7

*W*hen I was four years old, I had a significant experience of God. Some might question whether this was truly an authentic experience or just some figment of my imagination. Some might even wonder how it is possible that I could remember the experience after so many years. Yet for me, there is no question about it. The experience was real and remains fresh and vivid in my memory today.

It was one of those hot summer days, and I had been outside for most of the day playing with my friend from next door. We were hot and tired and dusty. The sun was going down and evening was falling. All at once, my attention was riveted upward to the beautiful sunset. I stood transfixed, eyes gazing on the gorgeous sight. The whole sky, it seemed, was encompassed with various shades of purple, pink, and mauve. My friend noticed that I was looking up and stopped her play to see what had caught my attention. As we gazed at this spectacular sight, we stood there in silence, awe-struck by the beauty of it all.

Finally she spoke to me in a whisper, "You know, don't you, that up there in the sky is where God lives?" Now I didn't know that, because to my knowledge I had never heard that bit of news before. However, not wanting to appear stupid, I remember that I said, also in a whisper, "Yes, I know that." I suppose this was one of the first lies I ever told!

Then she said, still in a hushed voice, "You know, don't you that the streets up there are paved with pure gold?" Again, I didn't know that, but for the second time, not wanting to appear dumb, I nodded my head yes. As we stood there for several more minutes, tears began to stream down my face. I had never experienced such a feeling before. The beauty, mystery, and awe of the moment overwhelmed me, and I felt God's presence in a very real way.

About that time, my mother called me to come inside for our evening meal. I suppose that my dirty face was tear-streaked because when I opened the door, she asked me why I had been crying. Not knowing how to express the feelings I had just experienced, I told another lie. I told my mother that I had mashed my finger in the door!

I believe that this experience is not too different from that of most children. They have experiences of God. They sense the awesome feeling of the Eternal. Yet, because they do not know how to express themselves or are afraid that they will be laughed at or misunderstood, they do not freely relate their experiences to others.

My husband, Tom, also had a vivid experience of God as a child. When he was nine years old, his grandmother became very ill and he was told that she was at the point of death. One of his childhood chores was to take the cow to the creek to get water. On this particular day, with his heart heavy with concern for his grandmother, he set out. When he arrived at the creek, he felt a special stillness about him. As the cow began to drink, he knelt down and began to pray for his grandmother to get well. He said that a peace came over him, and he felt God's presence in a very real way.

When I conducted a workshop on the Navajo reservation, I asked the adults there if they would be willing to tell about their first experience of God. Jackson Yazzie stood up and said that he would like to tell his experience. He said that his parents had left him and his older brother, Johnny, alone at their hogan (the

Navajo word for home or house). They lived among the hills far from the nearest trading post and his parents were to the trading post town to buy groceries and other supplies and would be gone overnight. They told the two boys to take good care of the sheep while they were gone.

Jackson said that he and Johnny began to play, as boys would do, and they forgot entirely about the sheep. As night began to fall, they remembered the sheep and began frantically to search for them. They ran from one mesa to another calling to the sheep. When they realized they were not going to be able to find them, Johnny said, "Let's just kneel down here in the ground and pray to the One who never dies, and ask Him to take care of our sheep." Jackson said, "We were actually praying to God, but at that time, we didn't know what to call God, so we just called him the 'One who never dies.' "

After they prayed, they went into the hogan and went to sleep. The next morning, just as day was breaking, they heard someone riding up to their hogan on a horse. A man got off his horse and called to the boys saying, "You boys come on over to my camp and get your sheep. They are all over there."

Jackson said that although that was a long time ago, he remembered this first experience of prayer as a time of feeling the power and presence of God. He continued to treasure the memory of it throughout his life. Many of the others at the workshop stood and related similar stories of encountering God in their lives at a very early age. The same is true of my conversations with adults from various other settings. All expressed the fact that they had had valid experiences of God when they were children. Some of these experiences were more vivid than others, but the majority of them felt that these were authentic experiences of God.

Many of the children I have interviewed also related touching stories of times when they had felt God's presence. For instance, Clint, age twelve, said that one night as he was in bed, lying very still and the house was unusually quiet, he felt God's presence with him. He actually felt that God was right there in the room with him.

Paige, age seven, said that the first time she felt close to God was when she was an "itty, bitty baby." She said that she was so close to God that she felt like she was hugging God. She continued by saying that she could just "barely remember when she was in heaven."

Ellie, age twelve, said that she felt especially close to God one Christmas Eve when she was at church. The nativity scene was so beautiful and the music so inspiring that she felt God was very close.

In 1963 Sir Alister Hardy, a "renowned British scientist, challenged his fellow scientists . . . to take seriously the fact of religious experience as a central feature of human life." In 1969 he founded the Religious Experience Research Unit at Manchester College, Oxford, and began extensive research on the subject. He collected the results of this research in his book *The Spiritual Nature of Man.*[1] Later, Edward Robinson became the director of the Religious Experience Research Unit and, as part of his research, many questionnaires were sent to adults, inquiring about their personal religious experiences. The responses flooded in and although no mention had been made of religious experiences that had taken place in childhood, many persons reported authentic religious experiences that had taken place when they were children. Many of the adults reported that these experiences were still very meaningful to them, many years after the event. From the data gathered, Robinson wrote a book called *The Original Vision: A Study of the Religious Experience of Childhood.*

Robinson concludes that children can have religious experiences. He says they have the insight, imagination, understanding and knowledge that enable them to have religious experiences. These qualities do not have to develop to some higher form, but are adequate to enable the child to experience God in just as valid a way as an adult. This conclusion differs drastically from the

developmentalists who feel that children move through stages
that are predictable, invariant, hierarchical, and universal.

The original vision that children have of God, Robinson feels,
is one that can only properly be understood when studied over a
period of time.[2] Perhaps its full impact will not be understood
until recollected later in life, but they are, nevertheless, experiences of the holy.

Somehow our system of education and our experiences in society, and even in our churches, have caused our early experience
of God, our "original vision," to fade. We have lost it somewhere
along life's journey. Our materialistic society and our striving
after position, power, and things have caused us to forget that we
are, indeed, spiritual beings. Robinson urges us to maintain this
original vision, because stored in the subconscious, it is able to
enrich our religious awareness at a later period when we are
ready for it.[3]

In his introduction to the American edition of Robinson's book
*The Original Vision*, John H. Westerhoof says, "Children should be
affirmed as persons who can and do have significant experiences
of the divine which, while only recollected and described later in
life, are still mature, mystical, numinous experiences of the holy.[4]

Along these lines, Neill Hamilton gives us some important
things to think about when he speaks of faith development. I
believe that what he has to say about the development of faith ties
in closely with our understanding of the child's view of God and
of the child's ability to pray to God.

In his book *Maturing in the Christian Life*, Hamilton offers a bib-
lical-theological version of faith development as an alternative to
the psychological version James Fowler gives in his book *Stages
of Faith*.[5] As we have said earlier, Fowler, in giving his six stages
of faith, draws heavily on Piaget's theory of cognitive development, Kohlberg's theory of moral development, and Erikson's
psychosocial development. Hamilton feels that Fowler's view of
faith and of the way that God enters human lives is a one-way
journey, moving from one lower stage to another until stage six is

reached.[6] He believes that Fowler is saying that "the track is pre-determined, but the degree of progression on it is not."[7] That is, a person may cease developing or get stuck in a lower level, never progressing farther along to a higher stage of faith. Hamilton says that although faith development may have stages or eras or sequence, "the life of faith is drawn ahead by the Spirit rather than driven from behind by the [psychological] self."[8] I agree that to view faith development solely from a psychological point of view totally leaves out the power and majesty of God.

What Hamilton is saying about faith development, I believe, helps us understand the spiritual potential of children and their first thoughts of God. These first impulses of God in the life of the child do not come as a result of the child's initiative but are the result of God's holy work in their lives. The child's first attempts at prayer are in response to a divine nudging from God.

The stages that have been identified so well by the developmentalists are important in child development, to be sure, but they in no way determine when and where and how the spirit of God enters the life of the child. The Holy Spirit surprises us in many places in our lives, and we do not know from where it comes or where it goes (John 3:8). We marvel at it and feel the result of its blessed presence.

Paul has said it so well, "For all who are led by the Spirit of God are children of God" (Romans 8:14). God is ever calling us and the children who are within our care into this divine-human relationship. Through prayer we are able to respond to this One who has created us and calls us into that joyful fellowship. This is why our own prayer life is important, and we must help our children learn to develop their own life of prayer. We, as adults in the child's life, can be a catalyst or a gateopener in this endeavor by helping to create time and space in which the wind of the Holy Spirit is allowed to blow where it will.

## CHAPTER FIVE

# Guidelines for Teaching Children to Pray

Thank you for food and shelter and my family and any other things. Thank you for friends. Thank you most of all for my family.

Jenna, age 8

Dear God,

Think you for this earth, and think you for the churches, and think you for the school and think you for our parents, and think you for our teachers that help us learn so we can get a education.

Shameka, age 8

*T*here are some important guidelines to remember as we consider the all important responsibility of guiding children in their prayer life. Initially we may be gripped with a sense of inadequacy when we think of the question, "Where and how do I begin?" Actually the task is not so overwhelming if we remember that we are not alone as we proceed. This cannot be said often enough. God is with us in our endeavors and the Holy Spirit gives us guidance. The foremost thing to strive for in prayer with children, as with adults, is to help them know that they can have a personal, ongoing relationship with God. We want them to know that God is the center of their lives. God is not something tacked on to Sunday or on to other special times, but God is with them as a constant and loving companion. God is like their best friend who loves them and understands them and can be trusted with anything that they want to say during their prayer time. God is there in the good times and the bad.

In helping children with their prayer life, remember to start with small beginnings, and from these small steps, larger steps can be taken. Remember also to begin where the child is and help the child move on from there.

## AT WHAT AGE DO WE BEGIN?

When should we begin to pray with our children? I believe we should begin praying with them before they are born. Music, for example, has been said to soothe a restless baby in the mother's womb. Could not prayer do the same? During the nine months of gestation, the parents, grandparents, and other loved ones should be constantly remembering the child in prayer.

Then from the time the child is born, continue to include the child in your prayer life, both at home and at church. As the special adults in the child's life, begin by offering prayers for your child or children when they are too young to pray for themselves. Gradually encourage them to begin praying themselves by saying simple prayers in their own words. Remember that one-sentence prayers are sufficient for young children.

Some people will perhaps argue against beginning to pray with a child at an early age. They may say, "How can a small child know what is being said in prayer? How can he or she understand?" These persons may feel that prayer can easily degenerate into a magical formula for a young child, as we have seen in chapter 3 on "Ages and Stages." Prayer does have the potential of becoming a religious game for the child, and God can become a giant Santa Claus in the sky. Nevertheless, I believe we should pray with our children as early as possible, understanding that they will go through various stages in their prayer life. They will grow in their perception and understanding of prayer, just as we as adults grow in ours. How do we begin?

The primary prayer experience for the young child is that of praise and thanksgiving. Simple prayers such as "Thank you, God, for this beautiful day," or "God, thank you for the beautiful flowers" are adequate and appropriate prayers for the young child. These prayers of thanksgiving are a natural response for the child and are an excellent place to begin. From this small beginning, as the child grows and develops, other types of prayers may be added. With time the child is able to pray other forms of prayer. Prayers of confession might be added such as "Help me be kinder to my brother" or "I'm sorry I was cross with my friend."

But remember that for the very young, their primary prayer experience is praise and thanksgiving.

## PRAY AS YOU CAN

A mother of a busy toddler asked me once how to pray with her child. "He won't be still, not even for one second," she said. "I've tried to get him to be quiet for a short, one sentence prayer, but he won't even stop for that." My response was, "Then pray with him on the run. As he is running in the yard, run beside him, and notice the flowers or the leaves or whatever catches his attention. Just comment on them, saying, 'God made such beautiful flowers or leaves.' Or say, 'Thank you, God, for making such a beautiful world.'" Even this small beginning will bear fruit.

## CALLING THE CHILD'S NAME IN PRAYER

As we pray, both with and for our child, remember to call the child's name in prayer. By doing this, we let them know that they are important to us and to God. This also helps the child see the importance of naming those they love in their own prayers.

I don't think any of us ever gets tired of hearing our name called in prayer. My husband has a friend who drops by his office occasionally. As she leaves, she often says, "Pray for me, Tom." And then after she has stepped outside the door, she usually sticks her head back in and adds, "And pray for me by name, Tom."

I remember distinctly the first time I can recall my mother calling my name in prayer. Perhaps she had done it many times before, but this time made a great impact on me. I was in the first grade and had ridden to school that day with my older cousin who had her own car. On the way, the door accidentally came open as we were turning a corner. I tumbled out and rolled under the car. (This was before cars had seat belts.) Fortunately my cousin was able to stop the car before it ran over my legs. As we had our prayer before dinner that evening my mother thanked God that I had not been seriously injured. Hearing my mother call my name in prayer made me feel her love and God's love.

In our nurseries at church, or in our infant's room at home, simple prayers may be offered on behalf of the babies in the cribs. The nursery worker at church, as he or she walks by the cribs, may say a word of thanks for each child, using their names. At home, as the baby is being put down for a nap or for the night, parents can offer a prayer aloud, using the child's name. To lay our hands on our children as we pray also gives them a sense of specialness and blessing. In a world filled with violence and turmoil, it is a wonderful thing to bless one another by laying hands on each other and offering a prayer of blessing.

Henri Nouwen says that the word blessing comes from the Latin word *benedicere*, or *benediction*. Benediction literally means speaking (*dicto*) well (*bene*) or saying good things of someone. He continues, "To give a blessing is to affirm, to say 'yes' to a person's Belovedness. And more than that: to give a blessing creates the reality of which it speaks."[1] We must convey to our children that they are the beloved of God, just as they are loved by us.

## ESTABLISHING PATTERNS OF PRAYER

The earlier we begin to pray with our children the better chance they have of feeling comfortable with prayer. Compare this idea to reading with our children. The earlier we expose them to books, the greater chance they have of becoming good readers. Perhaps the earlier we expose our children to prayer, the better chance they have of becoming persons of prayer. However, if you have not formed this practice early on, it is never too late to begin!

There is also something to be said about beginning good habits at an early age. The earlier good practices are learned, the better chance they have of becoming a good habit and establishing themselves in the child's life. In our culture, we have gotten away from the spiritual disciplines that our spiritual ancestors used, and somehow in the day in which we live, these disciplines of the spiritual life seem foreign to us. We know, however, that there is nothing that can take the place of established patterns of prayer, specific times for scripture reading, and set times of silence to be alone with God. John Wesley said long ago, "Whether you like it or no, read and pray daily. It is for your life." The earlier we learn this, the richer our lives will be. To teach our children to maintain these disciplines would be a great gift to them.

Mealtimes and bedtime are two important times of prayer with our children. In the interviews I conducted, I asked the children, "Can you remember the first time that you prayed?" Almost without exception they answered, "At home, with my mom or dad, before meals or before I went to sleep." These are crucial times for prayer with children. Other established times for prayer are worship times in Sunday school and in church. Special times of the year, such as Advent, Christmas, Lent, Easter, and birthdays should be times of prayer also. During these special times, there is much we can do with children to help them know God's love for each of them. Later, in chapter 7, we will look at some specific things we might do during these special times to enhance the child's prayer life.

## CHILDREN LEARN BY IMITATION

We know that young children learn a great deal by imitation. By watching us pray and by imitating us, children will see that prayer is a natural thing to do. Gradually they will develop a style of their own, even though in the beginning, they are imitating us in our prayer life. Just helping children know that they can express their feelings to God at any time and in any place and about any thing will lay a crucial foundation in prayer for them.

When our granddaughter was two years old, she and her parents went on a retreat with us. Her parents left early one morning, before Maggie was awake, to go for a hike. I was still in bed and was reading my Bible. Since I was too comfortable to get up to get my glasses, I had to hold the Bible at arm's length to see to read. After a few minutes, I heard the door creak and Maggie came toddling in. She climbed into bed with me without saying a word. She lay there for a few minutes watching me. Then she spotted my husband's Bible on the dresser, got out of bed quietly, reached up and got the Bible, and returned to her spot beside me. After she got settled again, she opened the Bible and thrust her little arms out, holding the Bible at arm's length, as I was doing, pretending to read. That said a lot to me about the power of imitation. Our actions may very well speak louder than our words.

## RITUALS AND REPETITION

Rituals have special importance for young children. Somehow rituals give them the feeling of security. Klink said that "if we do not invent ceremonies for children, they make them up themselves."[2] When we give children rituals, they don't have to invent their own to give them the reassurance and structures in life they need. The rituals we create are important to the child's spiritual growth.

It is important, also, to repeat phrases over and over again, and to pay attention to the rhythm and rhyme of the words we use with children.[3] This is not "vain repetition" in the eyes of the child! They love words that sound alike, and they enjoy the rhythm of repeated phrases. They do not grow tired of hearing the same words over and over as adults do. I remember vividly a stage our younger son, Tim, went through. Our bedtime prayers turned into a lengthy ordeal as Tim entered the stage when he enjoyed hearing and using words that rhyme. After the usual "God bless Mama and Daddy," he then began asking God to bless everyone he could think of whose name began with the letter "H." "God bless the Holyoaks, the Holtzs, the Heights, the Howards, the Hughes, the Heffelfingers" and the list went on and on. We were also reading "Winnie the Pooh" about that time so the "Heffalump" got in there too! This type of prayer is to be expected with children and should be cherished as something to remember with joy after the children are grown. God certainly understands this type of prayer, and I believe thoroughly enjoys it!

## TEACH CHILDREN TO USE THEIR OWN WORDS IN PRAYER

Encourage children to use their own words in prayer to God. For God to hear them, they don't have to use our adult language or the traditional prayer language of the church, beautiful as it is. We don't ever want to extinguish their spontaneous expressions to God. Prayers learned by heart are fine; but spontaneous prayers in the child's own words are very acceptable to God. I prefer the term "learned by heart" rather than "memorized" because to memorize seems to me to be a rote process, whereas to learn by heart connotes that the heart is involved in remembering the words, not just the head.

Sometimes children get words mixed up in their prayers, and they may use words or phrases that make us want to laugh. I believe that God has a great sense of humor and understands completely what the child means to say. Recently at our church, a Sunday school teacher asked the children to mention something in their prayer for which they were thankful. Brandon said, "Thank you, God, for dust. Thank you for this time of dust that we are celebrating." After the prayer, the teacher called him aside and asked him about his prayer. "What is this time of dust you were talking about?" "Oh, you know, this time before Easter that we are celebrating." "You mean Lent?" his teacher asked. "Yeah, Lent," answered Brandon. I think even God had a chuckle over that one!

## CHILDREN CAN PRAY ANYTIME, ANYWHERE, AND SAY ANYTHING TO GOD

Children need to know that they can pray anytime, anywhere, under any circumstance, and say anything to God they want to say. Honesty is not hard for children! In fact, they are very good at it. When they think of prayer as talking with God who is a friend, they can then talk in normal ways to God about whatever is on their mind. Even though God does not talk back in audible language, this does not seem to be a problem with children. Tell children that God is big enough to handle whatever they want to say to God. Sometimes this frees them to pray about their innermost thoughts, about things that have been troubling them, or about personal issues that they have difficulty discussing with anyone else. These issues can be presented to God in confidence and trust.

Recently at a Wednesday night prayer service at our church, one father brought his seven-year-old son, Scott. After our time of lifting up the needs of persons in our congregation and of having a time of silent prayer at the altar, those present held hands and began to take turns praying short prayers. I was standing next to Scott, and when it came his turn to pray, I thought perhaps that I should skip him and begin my prayer. I was assuming that he would be embarrassed or would not feel comfortable offering a prayer. How wrong I was! Before I could begin praying, Scott, in his beautiful, childlike, spontaneous way, began to pray. He thanked God for the beautiful summer day and for all the beauties of nature. He thanked God for the privilege of attending a soccer camp daily that week. In closing, he asked God to help him do his best at the camp every day. These were the things that were on his mind, and he felt comfortable bringing them to God in prayer. To be secure enough to bring to God all of our needs and desires is one of the main goals in prayer.

## POSTURES OF PRAYER

Children also need to know that there are a variety of postures for prayer. At times we close our eyes, but this does not always have to be the case. At times bowing our heads is appropriate. Other times we might want to just sit quietly. Sometimes we might want to kneel, and other times we might want to stand with our arms outstretched. We might even feel led to pray lying face down on the floor with arms outstretched, making the sign of the cross. To use various postures in prayer brings a vitality to our prayer life and to the child's.

## PRAYERFUL THOUGHTS

As has already been stated, spontaneous prayers are always appropriate when you are with a child. A beautiful rainbow or a gorgeous sunset observed, naturally leads to prayer. You might pray quietly, "Thank you, God, for the beauty all around us." You also might say something like this: "Isn't God good to make such a beautiful rainbow?" This is a form of prayer that might be called "prayerful observations" or "prayerful thoughts." It is simply stating a prayer thought, and this type of prayer focuses on God and on God's great care of us.

## SPECIAL PLACES OF PRAYER

Children need to know that they can pray anywhere, but they can also have special, private places of prayer. Marlene Halpin says that children should find the place in their house that fits them and let this be their special place of prayer.[4] Special places mean a great deal to children and having their own place of prayer is exciting for them. Help them to understand that they can pray in their private place, but also they can pray anywhere.

Their special place of prayer can be under a bed or in a closet or behind a door or just beside their bed. Suggest that the child put things that have a special meaning in his or her special place of prayer. This might be things from nature that remind them of God, such as a feather, a bird's eggshell, a pretty rock, or a small flower vase with a flower or two. (For obvious reasons, unless supervised, candles should be discouraged!) Such items chosen by the child makes the place the child's own and should be respected by other members of the family as a sacred place.

## PRAYER IS LISTENING TO GOD

Many times children ask the question, " How do I hear God speak to me?" or "Does God talk out loud?" or "How do I know that God has really spoken to me?" Often, we as adults, ask the same questions, if not audibly, at least in the deep recesses of our hearts. We wonder how we can recognize God's voice when it comes, and we too struggle with what it means to hear the voice of God.

Few of us have actually heard the audible voice of God coming to us with an answer to prayer. Some people attest to the fact that they have, indeed, heard the voice of God speaking to them; but for most of us, this is not the case. Help children understand the ways God speaks to us today. If children know and understand the various ways God speaks to us, they can then more readily discern the voice of God speaking to them.

How does God speak? God speaks to us in the quiet of our own hearts. After we have prayed about some issue, we may feel a sense of calm, a certain peace about the situation for which we prayed. An answer comes to us out of the quiet and we recognize this as the voice of God.

Sometimes we pray about a direction we should take. Perhaps both ways seem equally good, but a choice has to be made, and we feel confused. We go to God in prayer and suddenly in the silence, as we earnestly seek God's will for us, one of the options seems to loom larger than the other. There is a sense of rightness about it and peace comes over us. We recognize this peace as the voice of God, speaking to us in answer to our prayer.

As children mature, they will find that God often speaks to them just as God does to adults, through friends and loved ones. Perhaps we are praying about something, earnestly seeking a word from God. Then as we talk with a friend or loved one, he or she will say just the thing we need to hear. Perhaps it is a word of comfort or a word of encouragement, or perhaps it is a word of direction or a word of advice, but it comes to us as the voice of God. Again, calmness comes to us, and we know that we have heard the voice of God.

Also, as children mature and are able to read their Bibles, they will come to see that God often speaks to them through the Living Word. A verse of scripture will come to them as a direct response to something for which they have prayed.

God is able to speak to us in various ways. We must develop listening hearts so that we will hear the voice of God when it comes, in whatever form it takes.

## PRAYING THE PRAYERS OF OUR FAITH

The common prayers that we pray together as Christians are special to the community of faith and are extremely important for children to learn. Many of these prayers have come to us through the centuries and are a great part of our religious heritage. Some of the prayers will stay with the child forever and will not have to be discarded later in life because they have "outgrown" them. A good example of this is having children learn to pray the Lord's Prayer even before they can fully understand the words. Praying the Lord's Prayer with others in a worship service can be a powerful experience for the young child.

David Kerr tells the story of the time when he was the visiting evangelist at a large camp meeting. He preached every night, and during the afternoons he visited the families who had come for the week of services. As he visited one family, the mother of several children commented that one of the young boys was not hers but was a friend of one of her sons and had come with them for the week. She explained that this was a new experience for the boy as he had never before been to church. David made a special effort to talk with the boy whose name was Mark. One evening, as David was sitting alone on the front pew awaiting his time to preach, he felt someone come quietly and sit down beside him. When he turned, he saw that it was Mark who had come forward by himself to sit with him. David smiled and welcomed the child. As the service began, the song director led them in singing the great songs of the faith. Obviously Mark did not know the hymns, but he carefully held his song book and did his best to keep up with the words. Following the hymn sing, someone came to lead the congregation in prayer. At the close of the prayer, everyone was asked to join in praying the Lord's Prayer. As the final "Amen" was said, Mark, with eyes very wide, punched David on the arm and asked excitedly, "How did you know that?" Mark looked around at the congregation, waved his hand towards them and asked in astonishment, "How did they know that?" Later in relating the story to a small group of worshipers, David asked the questions, "How are the children to learn the prayers of our faith unless we teach them? If they have never heard a mother or a father or a grandparent pray, how will they ever know how to pray?"[5] Praying together the ancient prayers of our faith is a powerful experience, and children are quick to recognize the feeling of awe that it brings. At first, they might not fully understand the words, but in time, they will come to understand what they mean.

## GOD ANSWERS PRAYERS

Children need to know that God answers prayers. The answers may be different from the way we have prayed. This is sometimes troubling to children. Of course, we always want all of the prayer experiences of children to be positive ones, but we cannot be sure that will happen. When a child prays for a sick loved one to get well, and the person dies, the child might come to believe that God either didn't hear his prayer or did not answer it. This might cause great pain and confusion in the child. Sometimes these issues are hard to work through.

Children need to understand that God answers prayers in different ways just as their parents answer their children's requests for things in different ways. God sometimes says "yes," sometimes "no," sometimes "wait awhile," and sometimes "I have a better way;" but always God says "I am with you in this, no matter what."

Thus we must help the child form positive concepts about God early in life. During difficult times, the child is comforted and helped if she believes that God is good and that God loves her. If children hold the concept that God knows what is best for them and cares about them infinitely, no matter how the prayer is answered, they will have the assurance of God's presence and love.

Delia Halverson, in her book *How Do Our Children Grow?* suggests that we include community helpers in the prayers of children. You might encourage them to pray, "Help the doctor to help my grandmother get better."[6] Assist children to understand that although doctors are God's helpers, sometimes they don't discover what's wrong soon enough to make the person well, or maybe no one has found the right medicine yet.[7]

Personally, I would not discourage a child from praying for his or her loved one to get well. All of us who have had loved ones who are ill know that to pray for their healing is a normal instinct. We all want miracles even though we know that they might not come. And so we pray for healing; and Jesus' life and message teach us that this is certainly an acceptable, even a desirable form of prayer.

My daughter, Suzanne, who is an ordained minister and has worked as a chaplain in a hospital, has helped me with this. She said when she first began her work in the hospital, she felt torn when terminally ill persons asked her to pray for their healing. Would she be giving false hope to pray for the person's healing? Would she be giving the family false hope? When she spoke with her supervisor about her concerns, the supervisor said, "Certainly pray for their healing if they ask you to or if you feel led to do so. We are not gatekeepers on God's healing. God heals as God chooses. It is not up to us to decide who can be healed and who cannot."

For this reason, and because I believe that God can and does heal, I would never discourage anyone from praying for the healing of a loved one. With children, however, I would be very careful to explain that for many reasons, and sometimes for reasons that we do not understand, persons are not always healed in this life. But reassure them that no matter how the prayers are answered, they can be assured that God loves them very much and is always with them.

## PRAYER LEADS TO ACTION

Children need to know that prayers often lead to action. Doing one's part in bringing about the answers to prayer is something God expects and needs us to do. We are a part of God's great plan, and our helping hands are essential if God's reign is to come on this earth.

Some time ago, I was working at a church when a hurricane hit off the eastern seaboard. The local news on the television was filled with images of the terrible destruction. There were pictures of children who were homeless and helpless. There were pictures of families waiting in long lines for fresh water and food.

The children in our church were impacted daily with these pictures of people in need. During a meeting with all the children one

Sunday morning, they prayed for these people. Later, the teachers in the Sunday school said that during worship times in their individual classrooms, the children continued to pray for the people in need.

Finally, one little girl suggested that we do something to help the families. After several suggestions were made, we decided to collect pennies for the people who were suffering the damage of the hurricane. We called the campaign, "Pennies for People in Peril." We obtained two very large clear plastic water jugs from a local distributor of bottled water and put them in strategic places in the church. Pennies began to pour in! The children brought them by the bags full. When the adults saw what was happening, they got excited about the effort, and they too began to bring pennies. Before it was over, we had collected over a thousand dollars for the relief effort.

Children need to know that they have to put "feet on their prayers" sometimes. God expects us to do our part for we are partners with God in helping to bring God's reign on earth. These, then, are some of the guidelines we must be aware of as we participate in helping our children learn to pray.

## CHAPTER SIX

# Forms of Prayer to Use with Children

Dear God,

Thank you for This wonderful day we have got and Thank you for answering our prayers. In Jesus name, amen.

Rachel, age 5

God of earth and God of light,

Have mercy on this soul who has not lived as so many times I have sung and prayed. Yet I am thankful for the morning and the night for in the morning my life can begin anew, and in the night I can pray for your forgiveness for the wrongs I have committed. I ask you for your love and forgiveness that I may live more like you want me to. Amen.

Mina, age 12

*T*he old adage "variety is the spice of life" has a certain significance for our prayer life. Many forms of prayer can be used, both for children and for adults, and these different forms or modes give variety as we grow in our prayer experience. Note, however, that prayer can never be reduced to a technique because prayer is not a technique, it is a relationship with God. Thus we are striving for ourselves and our children a vital, ongoing, personal relationship with the living Lord. This can be accomplished by talking with and listening to God, and various modes or forms of prayer can give richness and variety to our prayer experience.

## PRAISE AND THANKSGIVING

Prayers of praise and thanksgiving come naturally to children as they are quick to praise and to give God thanks for all that God has done. Therefore, praise and thanksgiving are wonderful places to begin our prayer journey and should be the primary prayer of younger children. Encourage them to use their own words. Short verses from the Psalms also are helpful when expressing praise and thanksgiving. Some of these may include Psalm 19:1, Psalm 9:1, Psalm 21:1, Psalm 34:1, Psalm 47:1, Psalm 92:1, Psalm 100:1-2, Psalm 107:1, and Psalm 118:24.

## CONFESSION AND REPENTANCE

As children get older, they can pray other forms of prayer. When children begin to realize that they have hurt someone by their words or actions, they can pray prayers of confession and repentance. To verbalize hurtful experiences to God in prayer is a catharsis action bringing a sense of cleansing to the person, whether a child or adult. It supports our belief that God is loving and forgiving when we do wrong. To be able to say to God, "I'm sorry that I hurt my friend" helps the child have the courage to say the same thing to the one who has been hurt.

Children also must learn to ask God to help them forgive someone who has done them wrong. Forgiveness is not easy for any of us, and it is considered by some of the saints to be the most difficult of the spiritual disciplines. Fortunately, children seem to be able to forgive far easier than adults. Children can be angry with a friend one day and then the next day, when adults would still be nursing a grudge, they can be seen on the playground with their arms around one another! A great lesson in the spiritual life is to learn how to say, "Help me forgive my friend who has done me wrong."

## PETITION AND SUPPLICATION

As the child matures, he or she can pray prayers of petition or supplication. These prayers are requests that are made earnestly and humbly of God about our own needs and desires. The word "supplication" may be described as "earnestly and humbly asking God for what we need or want." As the child begins to make requests, one should endeavor to help the child understand that although God doesn't always answer our prayers in the way that we had hoped, God always hears our prayers and answers them according to what is best for us. This is a hard concept for adults to understand; it is equally hard for children. When we reinforce that God is a loving God and wants the best for us, then we find peace in the answers that come.

## INTERCESSION

Another important form of prayer is the prayer of intercession. For several years, a young child focuses on her or his own needs. This is natural for a time, but as children grow and mature, they gradually begin to pray for the needs of others. This is the prayer of intercession—forgetting our own needs and focusing on the needs of another. One definition of the verb "to intercede" is "to plead on another's behalf." This is what the prayer of intercession truly is: to unselfishly and humbly pray for the needs of another.

Prayers of intercession seem to come easily for children. They begin by praying for their own family members, for relatives, for friends, for those whom they know intimately. From there, they begin to pray for those in need everywhere. Perhaps they have seen on television a story of a disaster somewhere in the world and they pray for that situation. Perhaps they have seen a picture on the front page of the local paper of a family who has lost its home in a fire and feel moved to pray for the family. These signs of growth should be encouraged and strengthened as the child matures.

## GUIDANCE

The prayer for guidance is another type of prayer. Throughout the Bible we have examples of persons who have sought God's guidance through prayer. In today's world, children have many crucial decisions to make. They are faced with temptations that children several years ago did not face. For example, they are confronted, at a very early age, with the temptation to use drugs and alcohol, and they are under enormous peer pressure. Although we hope that they depend on trusted adults to give them guidance, they should also learn to seek God's help when a decision has to be made.

How does God answer prayers for guidance, whether they are our own prayers or the prayers of a child? Often God uses a friend or family member to bring us the answer we have been seeking. Sometimes God sends the answer through the holy scriptures in a word or a phrase. And sometimes God answers in our own hearts, whispering a word of guidance so quietly that it is only heard by our ears. In Isaiah 30:21 we read ". . . your ears shall hear a word behind you, saying, 'This is the way; walk in it.'" This is often the way God brings guidance to our lives, but we must have listening ears to hear. Let us hope that our children will also learn to have listening ears.

## ADORATION

One short formula for prayer that children enjoy is the formula ACTS: Adoration, Confession, Thanksgiving, and Supplication. They are probably familiar with the words confession and thanksgiving, but may have to be taught what the word *adoration* means. (The word *supplication* has been discussed earlier.) We can explain that *adoration* is loving or worshiping God with the most profound or deepest love that one can imagine. It is being in awe of all that God is and all that God has done and worshiping (adoring) God for these many gifts.

One illustration might be of help here to distinguish the meaning of adoration from praise and thanksgiving. A father was seated at his desk one evening catching up on some work. The children of the household knew not to disturb their father when he was at his desk. Even so, the youngest child slipped quietly into the room. As the father continued his work, the young boy just sat there, quietly watching. Finally the father stopped his work and said, "What is it that you want, son?" "Nothing," responded the child. "I'm just looking and loving." That's what adoration is. It is "looking and loving" and being in God's presence.

The formula ACTS, then, may help children in remembering the various types or modes of prayer and to incorporate these in their prayer lives.

## BREATH PRAYER

Another form of prayer that children can easily learn is the breath prayer. This is an ancient form of prayer that has been used for centuries and is a short prayer of praise and petition. The breath prayer consists of two parts; one part being the favorite name we use for God. For children, the easiest name for God is God. As they better understand the attributes or qualities of God, then other names for God may be chosen; for example, Jesus, Teacher, Father, Holy Spirit, Lord, Creator, Shepherd, Eternal One, and so on. The second part of the breath prayer is made up of a need and should be phrased as a request or a petition. Suggest that the child sit quietly for a few minutes and think of a need in her or his life at the present moment. Perhaps the child needs to know how to handle an unpleasant experience at school, or a situation with a friend. A brief phrase related to one of these needs could make up the second part of the breath prayer. Examples might be "Dear God, forgive me," "God, help me," "God, surround me," or "Be near me, Lord Jesus."

The name for God may be placed at the beginning of the breath prayer or at the end, depending on how the words fit together. Saying the prayer over several times, first by putting the name for God at the beginning of the breath prayer and then saying it several times with the name of God at the end, will help decide which way sounds best. Children should also be aware of their breathing while they are saying their breath prayers, and this may take some practice. Eventually, however, it will become an automatic and effortless expression of praise and petition to God. The first portion of the prayer should be said while breathing in and the second portion while they are breathing out. Discipline and practice will help this become a useful and meaningful form of prayer, both for adults and for children. The breath prayer may be changed as needs change.

The breath prayer can be prayed at any time and under any circumstance. Gradually the child will become accustomed to using it often which is the purpose of this type of prayer. In 1 Thessalonians 5:16-17 we read, "Rejoice always, pray without ceasing, give thanks in all circumstances; for this is the will of God in Christ Jesus for you." And again in Ephesians 6:18 we read "Pray in the Spirit at all times in every prayer and supplication." To learn to pray without ceasing is difficult for most of us, but the breath prayer is one way to help us achieve this important discipline. The breath prayer enables one to pray without ceasing while outwardly one continues to carry on one's regular routine. For children, they delight in knowing they can pray without anyone knowing and that they can have a secret and special prayer between themselves and God.

## THE JESUS PRAYER

Another short breath prayer that can be prayed at any time and in any place and under any circumstances is the Jesus Prayer. This prayer comes to us from the Christian tradition of the East and has been used by Christians since the sixth century. The Jesus prayer grew out of a desire to pray without ceasing, and for hundreds of years has been used by countless people who wanted to have a deeper life of prayer. (For further reading on the Jesus Prayer, see *The Way of the Pilgrim* written by an anonymous nineteenth-century peasant; and, for a deeper explanation of both the Breath Prayer and the Jesus Prayer, see Ron DelBene's book *The Breath of Life*.)[1] When I have used this prayer with children, they are intrigued with it, because it is a very old prayer. I ask them to use their imaginations to speculate about all the different persons who, over the centuries, may have used this prayer. Most children have very vivid imaginations and can come up with wonderful stories about persons who have perhaps prayed the Jesus Prayer!

Children like this prayer, also, because of its rhythm and flow. They like the sound of it. The prayer, "Lord Jesus Christ, Son of God, have mercy on me, a sinner," is easy to say and lends itself well to repetition. There are several shortened forms of the Jesus Prayer such as "Lord Jesus Christ, Son of God, have mercy on me," or "Jesus Christ, have mercy," or "Jesus, mercy." I would omit the phrase "a sinner" when using this prayer with young children.

Although the breath prayer and the Jesus Prayer are extremely helpful prayers, they should in no way take the place of all other prayers. John Dalrymple says that "the truth is that we only learn to pray all the time everywhere after we have resolutely set about praying some of the time somewhere."[2] Therefore, other types of prayer should continue, including spontaneous prayer and prayers before meals and at bedtime.

## LITANY PRAYERS

Litany prayers are excellent to use with children, particularly with children who are reluctant to express themselves aloud in prayer. Some children are unable, for various reasons, to verbalize their own prayers but are willing to share in a short, set response. Litany prayers are usually one or two lines followed by a responsive word or phrase, and they usually revolve around a central theme. For example, in a thanksgiving litany, a leader or a child, might pray one or two sentences of thanksgiving saying something such as "Thank you, God, for the beautiful world you have given us," and the other child or children would respond after each sentence prayer with a brief response phrase such as

"We thank you, Lord." Other phrases such as "Bless the Lord," "Come, Lord Jesus," and "Praise the Lord" as well as single words such as *Shalom* or *Hallelujah* could be used as responses.

Explain the meaning of any words that might be unfamiliar to the children. Although they have possibly heard the words *Shalom* and *Hallelujah*, remind them that these are Hebrew words that have been used for centuries. *Shalom* is often used either as a greeting or a farewell and is understood to mean "peace," but in its fullest sense it means completeness or wholeness. *Hallelujah* means to give praise or thanksgiving to God (*Hallel* means "praise," and *jah* is short for "Jahweh," God.) Therefore, the word means, "Praise God."

A psalm could also be used as a litany with a child or an adult reading the verses and the other child or children responding with a phrase. One example might be Psalm 148:1-4.

> Praise the Lord!
> Praise the Lord from the heavens;
> > praise him in the heights!
> Praise him, all his angels;
> > praise him, all his host!"

Response: *Praise the Lord!*

> Praise him, sun and moon;
> > praise him, all you shining stars!
> Praise him, you highest heavens;
> > and you waters above the heavens!"

Response: *Praise the Lord!*

Some children enjoy writing their own litanies and then taking time to pray them together. Many children are very creative with this type of prayer, and they reveal deep thoughts when given the opportunity to express themselves. A litany prayer that was written by children at Calvary United Methodist Church in Durham, North Carolina, illustrates their creativity.

Come.
Response: *Lord, help us show kindness in all we do.*
I love You.
Response: *Lord, help us show kindness in all we do.*
Eat with us.
Response: *Lord, help us show kindness in all we do.*
Love us. Care for us.
Response: *Lord, help us show kindness in all we do.*

## FLASH PRAYERS

The flash prayer is another form of prayer that is excellent to use with children. Frank Laubach is credited with originating this type prayer, and there are many versions of it today. A flash prayer is one that all of us can use, because, even with our hurried lifestyles, we can spare a few seconds for a flash prayer. The process is very simple. When we see someone in need, we flash (send) a prayer in his or her direction. "Lord, be with that person. Give him (her) a sense of your presence." Or if we hear a fire engine going by or see an ambulance speeding on the highway, we can flash a prayer, "Dear God, be with the person who is sick or who has been injured." If we see someone who looks very sad, we can flash a prayer, "Holy Spirit, I don't know what the need is in this person's life, but give her (him) a sense of joy, knowing that you are with her (him)."

Children quickly pick up on this type of prayer, and after a little practice, they recognize many situations when flash prayers can be prayed. Persons who use this form of prayer attest to the fact that it brings remarkable results. Sometimes the sad person for whom we have prayed smiles, or if we have just flashed a prayer at someone who is angry, their anger leaves. Truly—as Alfred, Lord Tennyson wrote—"More things are wrought by prayer than this world dreams of."

## BLESSING PRAYER

The prayer of blessing is a type of prayer that perhaps is not used as often as it should be. This prayer can be used by adults in offering a blessing for children, by children offering a blessing for adults, and by children offering a blessing for other children. The phrase "to bless" is another term children might need help in understanding. Some persons may feel that the concept "to bless" should not be used with children because the meaning of the word is very hard for them to grasp. I believe that it is a viable word for children and with some explanation, they can understand and use it correctly.

In chapter 5 we discussed Henri Nouwen's words about blessing one another. Nouwen said that the word *blessing* comes from the word *benediction* which means speaking well or saying good things of someone. Some additional meanings of the word *bless* are "to invoke divine (God's) favor upon; to honor as holy; to confer well-being upon." All of us need this type of prayer. To have another offer a blessing invoking God's favor upon us gives us a sense of being in the presence of God. How it improves our day when someone does that for us! One way for us to use the prayer of blessing is to gently lay our hands on another's head and offer a short prayer on his or her behalf. We do not have to be a minister or another religious leader to do this for one another—and even a child can do it!

Young children are able to learn a one-line prayer to bless a brother or sister or parent. Words such as "God bless you" or "May the Lord bless you and keep you" are sufficient. Older children might add "May the face of the Lord shine on you and be kind to you. May the Lord turn toward you and give you peace" (Numbers 6:25, author's paraphrase).

Special times to offer a prayer of blessing are when someone is going away from home or when the family is going to bed at night. Children can offer a blessing for younger brothers or sisters and parents can offer a blessing for children as they leave for school.

Children can offer a blessing for parents as they leave for work. Prayers of blessings especially on birthdays to undergird the fact that the person having the birthday is very special indeed. Teachers can offer a blessing for those in their classes and, if verbal prayer is not allowed, silent blessings may be given. My granddaughter attended kindergarten at a church where the minister invited the children into the sanctuary once a week. They were encouraged to file by the minister as he silently laid his hands upon their heads in blessing. Maggie asked me once, "Why does he do that?"

I replied, "Why, he is saying 'Thank you, God, for Maggie.'"

"But he isn't saying it with his mouth," she protested.

"I know, but he is saying it with his heart," I assured her.

We can say so much with our hearts! And the touch of someone blessing us is a beautiful thing. How desperately we need to reassure one another that we are spiritual beings, and using the prayer of blessing brings this truth to our remembrance.

## MEDITATION AND SILENCE

The last form of prayer that we will discuss in this section is the prayer of silence. This type of prayer prepares us for meditation and contemplation; for without the ability to be silent, meditation and contemplation are not possible. Unfortunately many of us, both adults and children, have lost (if we ever had it!) the ability to be silent. Every moment of every day is, for far too many of us, filled to the brim with noise and busyness of some sort.

The Desert Fathers and Mothers who lived in the Egyptian desert during the fourth and fifth centuries have taught us that silence is an essential discipline in the spiritual life.* They have

---

*The Desert Fathers and Mothers were the early spiritual leaders who left their homes and entered the solitude of the desert seeking a deeper life with God. This was the beginning of the monastic life.

revealed to us that silence is primarily a quality of the heart, and because this portable sanctuary is located within us, we can take it with us wherever we go. What a gift we have!

Yet few of us realize that we have this gift. Our lives are too full and too busy. We are constantly bombarded with noise: televisions, videocassette recorders, compact discs, telephones, pagers, and appliances of all sorts. We must be intentional if we are to withdraw from the commotion around us and learn the prayer of silence. Children, especially, need to be given the opportunity to do this as it prepares them to be able to return to that inner sanctuary throughout life.

Begin very early to teach your children to appreciate silence. When young children awaken during the night, we can help them get in touch with their "inner sanctuary." After getting them a drink of water, or meeting whatever need they might have, hold them for a few minutes and say, "Let's just sit here together and be very quiet. God likes to use times of quiet to speak to us in special ways."

As children get older, read or tell them the story of Samuel and Eli in the Old Testament (1 Samuel 3). God spoke to Samuel in the silence of the night, and we can emphasize that God often speaks to us at night or in other times of quietness.

Without exception, the children I interviewed when asked, "Do you think it is easier to pray when there is noise or when it is quiet?" always responded, "When it is quiet." They cited the television and other noise as keeping them from hearing God speak. One young girl said that she couldn't hear God speak if there was so much as a potato chip crunching! We should keep reminding children to find their own quiet place. These special places, places that just fit them (Marlene Halpin's term) are places where God can meet them at any time. And in the silence, God can speak to them and to them only. If a group of children is in the room, each child can still find a quiet place, perhaps in a corner, under a table, or behind a door. Most importantly, a child can find a quiet place within, even though there are others around.

Delia Halverson suggests that after a time of quiet, while the children are still in their places, invite them to get to know the "really-really me" that is inside themselves. They should consider the question, she says, of what is the really-really me? "Is the really-really me your arm? Is it your foot? Is it your head? What part of you laughs and cries? What part of you loves, and what part of you feels great when you do something for someone else? That is the really-really you."

She continues, "Right now just God and the really-really you are in your heart. Let God love you. . . . Enjoy the love. Listen to what God may have to say to you."[3]

After a time of quiet close this experience with prayer, praying the Lord's Prayer or some other appropriate prayer.

Another meditative prayer experience children enjoy is using portions of scripture as a directed meditation. Stories such as Jesus feeding the five thousand (Matthew 14:13-21), the story of Zacchaeus (Luke 19:1-10), or Jesus blessing the children (Mark 10:13-16) would be good ones to use. Encourage the child or children to enter into the story as if they were there. Let them use their senses to experience the story: smelling the smells, seeing the beautiful landscape, touching the green grass or the edge of Jesus' garment, hearing the birds singing, the people talking, or the water rippling.

The prayer of silence probably has not been used enough with our children. Marlene Halpin says, "God finds us wherever and whenever [God] pleases. Sometimes [God's] choice of time and place coincide with ours . . . not always. . . . It's up to us to recognize [God's] presence, and respond as we will."[4] By creating times of silence in a child's life, we are providing hospitality for God's Holy Spirit to come.

These are some forms of prayer I have found to be helpful with children. There are others, of course, and as you explore the various possibilities, you may want to make a list of your own.

## CHAPTER SEVEN

# Activities to Enhance the Child's Experience of Prayer

Dear God,

Thank you for the many blessings that you have given us. Please help me use these blessings to help others. Forgive me for all the bad things I have done. Amen.

Taylor, age 10

*O*ne of the most important things that has already been said about prayer, and cannot be said often enough, is that prayer is not a technique or a specific form or a certain activity. Prayer is a relationship with God—an ongoing, loving, personal communion with God. However, because young children cannot think abstractly, as adults are able to do, we must use various experiential activities to reinforce in as many ways as possible the meaning of prayer. Some activities that may be done either in the family at home or in classes at church will follow. In doing each of these, help the child understand the purpose of the activity, otherwise the activity is only that—an activity, not a prayer.

## THANK-YOU BOOK

One activity for very young children is making a "thank-you book" indicating things for which they are thankful. Let the children look through magazines and cut out (sometimes with help) pictures of things for which they want to thank God. These can be glued on pages and made into a book. The adult who is helping the child can encourage the child to pray a simple prayer of thanks to God, mentioning the items in the child's book. Older children might want to draw their own pictures rather than cut them from magazines. They can then add a single sentence of thanksgiving for each item in their book. They too should be given the opportunity to offer a prayer of thanksgiving to God for the things that they have illustrated.

## PRAYER BOX

A similar activity that reinforces prayers of thanks is making a "Thank-You Box." Cover and decorate a box of any sort, leaving a slot in the top. Children who are old enough might write on a slip of paper things for which they are thankful. These can be placed in the box. Younger children could, again, cut out their pictures from a magazine. At an appointed time, such as, during the evening meal if this is used in the home or at the worship time if it is used in Sunday school or other group settings, the children are invited to take a slip of paper or picture from the box, offer a prayer for whatever is shown or described. Everyone else would respond, "Thank you, God."

A variation of the "Thank-You Box" is a "Prayer Need Box" or "Family Prayer Box." This works especially well in the family as it encourages persons to share their needs without "making a big deal" out of it. Some in the family might be hesitant to talk about their needs but would be willing to write these down and put them in the box. Family members would know to check the box often and when there is a need, to pray for the one who wrote it.

Another activity lifting up the attitude of thanksgiving is for each child, either at home or in Sunday school or another setting, to make a treasure box. This could be any sturdy box. Encourage children to put in the box special things that remind them of God. Examples might be a feather, a rock, a part of a bird's eggshell, a dried flower, and the like. My children had boxes like these when they were small, and it was always interesting to see what items they chose to remind them of God and of God's goodness to them.

## COLLAGE

Children enjoy making collages, either individually or working with other children. They can cut out pictures of things for which they are thankful and glue them in some design on construction paper or poster board. Again, a prayer of thanks should be offered at the close of the activity.

## JOURNAL

As children get older, encourage them to develop a journal. Almost all children, when they are old enough, like to keep a diary which chronicles the daily events in their lives. A journal differs from a diary in that instead of telling of daily events, it tells of the person's interaction with God's presence in his or her life. Each child should have his or her own book. This might be anything from an inexpensive spiral notebook to a nicely bound book with blank pages and a pretty cover. Having a book with the pages lined will make it easier for children to write. The children should be assured that this is their private book. Whatever they write will be just between themselves and God. Some of the things they might include are portions of the Psalms or other Bible verses that are meaningful to them. Dried flowers or other items from nature may be added. Someone has said that for every miracle in our lives, we should write a psalm. This is a wonderful exercise for all of us, and the child with whom you are working should be encouraged to write her or his own psalm or other words praising God's goodness.

A prayer journal is also a helpful discipline if we are serious about our prayer life. Many adults, who want to deepen their prayer life, keep prayer journals and realize that this is helpful in keeping their prayer life on track. I believe that many children, also will find this a very meaningful tool.

There are many variations of a prayer journal, but the simpler the better for children. In the child's book, divide the page into four columns. Column one would be headed "Date." Column two would be headed "Person or Thing prayed for." If a person is being prayed for, the specific need should be included. Column three would read "Date God Answered." And column four would be headed "How God Answered."

This type journal does many things for us as we grow in our prayer life. First, it helps us see, that God does, indeed, answer our prayers. Sometimes we pray for someone or something and forget to notice that God actually answered our prayer!

Second, a prayer journal helps us see how God answers our prayers: sometimes God answers our prayers in ways that we had not prayed for or expected; God may have said "no." God may have answered our prayer in just the way that we had hoped; or God may have answered in a different and better way than we could have ever imagined. In some cases, when we look at the date of our prayer and then notice nothing is written in the two columns "Date God Answered" and "How God Answered," we realize that sometimes God says "Wait." Much patience is required when God says to us, "Wait." Strong persons of faith, who have a deep prayer life, attest to the fact that they have prayed, sometimes, for many years, before receiving an answer to their prayer. Help children see that this happens with our prayers too sometimes. Reassure children that God does indeed hear their prayers, and, in God's time and way, they will be answered.[1]

## STUDYING AND PRAYING THE PSALMS

A study of the Psalms also helps children grow in their prayer life. Explain to the children that the Psalms are very old, written many years before Jesus' life on this earth, and were read and prayed by Jesus. Included in the Psalms are songs and prayers, written by different authors expressing many different feelings. Read some of the psalms with the children and discuss the feeling and concern being expressed. Just as the authors of the Psalms expressed their feelings to God unashamedly, so can we today. God is big enough to understand and accept all our feelings, even feelings of sorrow, loneliness, fear, and anger.

Another way to help the child have special feeling about the Psalms is for them to select and write portions of them on individual pages. Suggest that the child illustrate the psalms and place them in a notebook where he or she can refer to them at any time. Children can use portions of the Psalms as prayers and learn to pray the Psalms, as has been done by many Christians before us.

Many of these verses may be learned by heart so that, in later years, the verses will come back to the child as a gift.

## MUSIC AND MOVEMENT

Songs also may be prayers, and children, especially, enjoy using their singing voices to praise God. Singing a few short lines of a song is an excellent way to help bring the child into the presence of God. Some of these might be "Jesus, Remember Me," "Alleluia," "Kum Ba Yah," "Every Time I Feel the Spirit," "Lead me, Lord," "Thank You, Lord," "This is the Day," and of course, there are many, many others. Church hymnals usually have a section in the index entitled "Prayer," "Prayer Responses," or "Children's Choir Selections" and Sunday school curriculum resources are an excellent source of songs appropriate for use with children.

Children enjoy movement in any form and are often delighted to learn that movement may be used in prayer. Suggest that children sway or dance to express their prayers to God. Let them use strips of lightweight, colored cloth or crepe paper to twirl in the air to the rhythm of music or silently as they pray. Let them know that they can use their bodies as well as their voices and minds to express praise. Children can make a prayer stick by taking an old broomstick (without the broom part) and attaching to one end of it a metal coat hanger turned upside down. Straighten the hook part of the hanger and tape it with masking tape to the broom-stick. Attach long, lightweight pieces of cloth or crepe paper to the long straight part of the hanger. Bells can also be attached to add another dimension. Suggest the children move the prayer sticks to express their feelings as they pray.

Other sounds can be added during prayer time by using simple musical instruments such as sand blocks, sticks, tambourines, and so forth. And of course, children love the sound of all these things!

## DISCOVERING JESUS' TEACHINGS ON PRAYER

For older elementary children, including grades three through six, an exciting project is to read and explore Jesus' teachings on prayer. Encourage the children to discover how many times Jesus prayed, where Jesus prayed, and under what circumstances he prayed. Children also may act out these situations, draw pictures to illustrate the events, or make and use puppets to tell the stories.

## DISCOVERING PRAYERS IN THE BIBLE

In addition to reading the prayers of Jesus, older children enjoy finding and reading some of the other prayers from the Bible. These might include Abraham's prayer for a son (Genesis 15:1-6), Daniel's prayer for wisdom (Daniel 2:17-23), David's prayer for blessing (2 Samuel 7:18-29), David's prayer for guidance (2 Samuel 2:1), Elijah's prayer for triumph over Baal (1 Kings 18:36-38), the Christians' prayer for Peter while he was in jail (Acts 12:5-12), the Disciples' prayer for boldness (Acts 4:24-31), Paul's prayer for the healing of Publius' father (Acts 28:8), Paul's prayer for grace (2 Corinthians 12:8-9), and Peter's prayer for the rais-ing of Dorcas (Acts 9:40). Help the children know the story behind each of these prayers and study them in order to better understand why the specific prayer was prayed.

## AMERICAN SIGN LANGUAGE

One exciting activity for older elementary children is learning American sign language to pray the Lord's Prayer. I have never seen children do this without personally having a deeply moving religious experience. I feel that it has the same effect on children when they take seriously what they are doing.

Books on how to do this are available in most libraries, but if you cannot find a written account on how to do this, locate someone who translates for the deaf who could help you. When the children have mastered the technique, have them share it with someone else, perhaps another class if this is learned in a church school class or with other members of the family if learned at home. Be sure the children know they are sharing a prayer and must convey an attitude of reverence.

## PHOTOS

Many children live hundreds of miles from their extended families and need to be reminded often of the love that flows between these relatives and themselves. Praying for each other is one way to bring this about. To know loved ones are intentionally praying for her or him, brings the child a sense of security.

Provide pictures of the different relatives in a photo album for each child. Every night, the child can look at the photos and offer a prayer for each loved one.

This worked very well for my family when we were living outside the United States for some years. Our son Mark had pictures of his grandparents, aunts, uncles and cousins in an album, and every night we would look at the pictures together and offer a prayer for them. My husband's parents came to visit us after we had been away one year, and Mark ran to them as if they had never been apart. I believe that prayer can bind us together no matter how many miles are between us. This is important for children to know.

## PRAYERFUL TOUCHES

Encourage children to pray for others in the world. Have available an inflatable globe, a regular globe, or a large map of the world. When something happens anywhere in the world, help them locate the place on the map or globe. Children can then offer a prayer by placing their hands on the country or place for which they are praying.

## PRAYER BRACELETS

Another tangible way to remind us to pray for a specific person or thing is by using a prayer string or bracelet. My grandmother had a way for remembering important things—she tied a string around her finger! This is not a bad idea in our prayer life. If we are remembering someone special in prayer or praying for some particular thing, tie a string around your finger or the child's finger to help her or him remember. Every time we notice the string, we are called to prayer.

A variation of this technique is to have a prayer bracelet. These can be made easily by plaiting three different colors of embroidery thread together to make a bracelet long enough to go around the child's wrist. The child can then whisper a prayer when they see the bracelet and remember the need. Practice makes perfect, and this is another way to encourage the child to pray anywhere, anytime, and about anything. All of life is holy; it cannot be divided into the secular and the sacred, and prayers are accepted by God at any time.

## PRAYER CHAIN

Making a prayer chain is another prayer activity that children enjoy. We have all made paper chains, and children love to make them too. Cut out, or let the children cut, equal-sized strips of paper for the chain. Let the children take each strip and write on it a prayer need, either for themselves or for someone else. After they have done this, they can glue the strips together to form a chain. Let them hang the chain in their room or wherever they choose.

## CELEBRATIONS

Special times in the child's life are times to emphasize prayer. Children's birthdays and the anniversaries of their baptisms are unique times to celebrate. Have birthday candles on the cake, certainly, but also have a large, special birthday candle which is lighted each birthday. Say a prayer of thanksgiving and blessing for the child, mentioning some of the good things that have happened in the life of the child during the previous year.

The anniversary of the child's baptism is an opportunity to have a similar ritual. Light a candle and give the child a chance to remember her or his baptism. Remind the child that through the sacred act of baptism he or she has been made a part of the community of faith. God's gift of love has made all this possible, and through the water and the Holy Spirit the child is claimed for God. If desired, read the story of Jesus' baptism (Matthew 3:13-17, Mark 1:9-13 or Luke 3:21-22). Show the child her or his certificate of baptism and offer a special prayer on the child's behalf. As has been said before, rituals are very important in the life of the child, and the significant events should certainly be celebrated with some ritual.

To celebrate Thanksgiving, use a special prayer calendar. A regular calendar might be used or, as a family, you might want to make a calendar with construction paper drawing in the days for November. Decide what you want to pray about during the month of November and write something special on each day. Or make the calendar like an Advent calendar. Cut around each day on three sides, leaving the paper attached at the top, so that it can be lifted up. Let children cut out pictures to be glued underneath. Every day, as a day is lifted, offer prayers of thanksgiving for whatever has been designated.

Advent, Christmas, and Easter offer rich opportunities to emphasize prayer and the sacredness of life. Because Christmas and Easter have become so commercialized, we must work hard in our families to keep the spiritual significance of these holy seasons. The Advent season begins four weeks before Christmas and begins a time of preparation for Christ's birth. During Advent, use an Advent calendar to mark the days leading to Christmas. These calendars can be easily and inexpensively bought or the family could make their own by following the instructions given above for making a Thanksgiving calendar. Every day during Advent, the spiritual nature of Christmas should be emphasized in some way.

An Advent wreath is another way to mark the sacredness of the season. Buy or make a wreath from a styrofoam ring and add either fresh or artificial greenery. The wreath requires four candles, three purple ones for royalty and one pink one for joy. On the first Sunday of Advent light the first purple candle, read from the scripture, sing a song, and prayer together. Continue this ritual each Sunday, relighting the first candle and lighting another purple candle on the second Sunday of Advent; relighting the two purple candles and the pink one on the third Sunday; and the final purple candle, along with those previously lit, on the Sunday before Christmas. On Christmas place a white Christ candle in the center of the wreath and light it along with the four candles.

As these candles are lit on Christmas, take time to read the Christmas story from the Bible and offer a prayer to God, thanking God for the birth of Christ, the light of the world. The children may take turns lighting the candles and participate by reading the scripture or offering a prayer.

Another way to keep the sacredness in Christmas is to have a nativity scene that is made of a material that is user-friendly for children. Children like to handle the nativity pieces and to rearrange them from time to time. This is good, because the more they are involved in Christ's birth event, the more they feel a part of it. The first nativity scene our granddaughter, Maggie, had was tiny. She was about three years old and enjoyed carrying it around with her, placing it first on one table and then another. We had a time of panic that year when, three days before Christmas, she couldn't find baby Jesus! We turned the house upside down and finally found the tiny piece between the sofa cushions!

Continue to remind children that Christmas is celebrated because it is Christ's birthday. Some families have a birthday cake for Jesus on Christmas to emphasize the true meaning of the day. These things help to offset the materialism of the season.

Lent and Easter offer another season rich in Christian symbolism. Lent begins forty days before Easter, not counting Sundays, and starts on Ash Wednesday. These forty days give us a wonderful span of time to talk about the symbols of Easter. Children should be taught that Easter eggs, bunnies, lambs, chicks, white lilies, and new clothes are all symbols for new life.

Many rituals in families may be established related to the season of Lent and Easter. In our family, throughout the years, we have observed several of these rituals, and they have made our lives much fuller. These traditions mean a great deal to children, and once they are started, children are not quick to give them up!

Two activities that became rituals for our family were making hot cross buns for Easter morning and a lamb cake for Easter dinner. Hot cross buns can be made of any sweet yeast dough, and after they are cooled slightly, a cross can be made with icing across the top. Some say that the custom of making hot cross buns dates back many years when a monk baked them to give to the poor on Easter morning. For many Christians, the custom has continued ever since. Children enjoy this activity and it gives them a different perspective from wondering what the Easter bunny is going to bring them or what they will wear on Easter morning. Explain to young children why you are making a cross on the top.

For many centuries the lamb has been an important Christian symbol. Whereas in the Hebrew religion the lamb was used as a sacrifice, in the Christian faith Jesus became the sacrifice and is often referred to as "The Lamb of God." Years ago, making a cake in the shape of a lamb became a ritual in our family and has continued, even though on several occasions, it did not look much like a lamb. In fact, some years the children referred to it as "the weasel cake," but yet we continued to make it. Try as I might to stop making it after the children were older, if it was not on the table for dessert on Easter, they invariably asked, "Where is the lamb cake?" With young children, I would not use the concept of Jesus being a sacrifice. It is enough to say that because Jesus is called the Lamb of God, we use the lamb as a symbol for Easter.

Another ritual that might be established on Easter is to light a white Christ candle on Easter Sunday, either during the main meal or at some other appropriate time during the day. For children, the thought of the crucifixion is a terrifying thing and must not be dwelt upon. In fact, when it is mentioned, as it must be sometimes, we should immediately follow a statement about the crucifixion with the statement that Jesus did not stay dead. God had a better plan and brought him back to life to be the light of the world. The Christ candle symbolizes this light for all of us. These are activities that can be used in our homes or in other locations to reinforce our prayer experiences with children. You will undoubtedly add others as you help the special child or children in your life grow in their prayer experience.

# CHAPTER EIGHT

# And a Little Child Shall Lead Them

Thank you Lord for being there for me when I need you most. And thank you for guiding me through the darkness of life, for without you I'm blind and I see nothing unless you tell me the way. And thank you for letting me be able to act as close to you as you allow, for I too want to be good.

Elizabeth, age 12

*I*n the book of Isaiah we read the often quoted lines: "The wolf shall live with the lamb, the leopard shall lie down with the kid, the calf and the lion and the fatling together; and a little child shall lead them" (Isaiah 11:6).

Isaiah's vision, which is actually God's vision for the world, is beautiful indeed. In actuality, however, this vision is a far cry from the world in which we live. In Isaiah's description, the wolf and the lamb who are natural enemies, will live together in peace. The leopard and the lion will no longer be threats to the weaker creatures in nature. The little child will be able to be the shepherd, because all in creation will live together in harmony and peace.

How we long for this vision of the realm of God! We desperately want to put violence, vicious crimes, homelessness, child neglect and abuse, brokenness, illness, and pain behind us. We would so like to live in this peaceful kingdom that Isaiah describes where even the child is safe, and old enemies live in harmony with one another. And yet we have to admit that this is not the world in which we live.

Perhaps, though, there is much we can learn from Isaiah's vision. The little child in our midst is a symbol and a sign of hope of the coming reign of the realm of God. The child is an eschatological presence—one that gives us a foretaste of the coming reign of God's kingdom in which we will all sit together in peace at the table of the Lord and feast at the heavenly banquet prepared for us. It is the child who will lead us toward this new vision, giving us a momentary glimpse into God's hope for the world.

Many times we underestimate the ability or the potential of children in our society. For instance, when we think of children, we often think of them as learners, but the reality is that children are not only learners, they are teachers as well. Just as we help them learn about prayer and the spiritual life, they, in their own way, are equally our spiritual guides and mentors. They bring the spirit of God into our midst.

Recently I changed the focus of my ministry. I had been working in a church for several years, and a great deal of my work was with children. In my new job I began working primarily with adults. Although I loved my new situation and felt that I was where I should be, I wondered why I had such a sense of loss and sadness. I felt as if I were going through a grief process. Various emotions filled me daily.

Finally I realized what the problem was. I missed the children! For several years, they had enriched my life in ways that I had not even been aware. Just hearing their voices at play or having a small child wave to me and call my name or feel one of them grabbing me around my legs with a quick hug had nourished my soul. I believe nothing can take the place of these rich, life-giving encounters with children.

In thinking of the role that children play in our spiritual journey, we might ask the question, "In what ways do children serve as spiritual guides for us?" I believe they do this for us in several identifiable ways. Children, because of their innocence, are closer to the mysteries of life than the rest of us. They can teach us, if we let them, to live in wonder of all that God has created. To see everything with the eyes of the child brings to us again a profound sense of awe and amazement.

I am reminded of the story a friend told me not long ago. On a beautiful spring day, she and her little girl had taken a long walk in the country. They left the road and wandered through a wooded area, and as they emerged from the woods, they found themselves in a beautiful meadow. The meadow was filled with wild flowers, almost as tall as the child. The child was delighted with the beauty of the place and ran on ahead of her mother through the beautiful flowers. As the mother followed, she heard some distance ahead of her in the midst of the flowers, the little girl singing:

> Fair are the meadows,
> fairer still the woodlands
> robed in the blooming garb of spring;
> Jesus is fairer, Jesus is purer,
> who makes the woeful heart to sing.[1]

The mother said that this was a rich, spiritual experience for her, and she truly felt God's presence.

Some years ago, when our children were young, we moved to the Southwest. The children were very excited and spent the first days in their new home exploring and marveling at all the wonderful things they were seeing for the first time. One late afternoon, our son Tim who was three years old at the time, was playing in the yard. Suddenly the door burst open, and he rushed in exclaiming, "Come quick and see, Mom. The sunset is all over the place." Indeed, those southwestern sunsets are something to behold, and as I ran outside and viewed the sky, a sense of wonder and awe filled me. If Tim had not called my attention to it, I probably would not have noticed the sunset. I was too busy unpacking boxes.

Much of life is like this. We miss the important things of nature because we are doing something mundane like unpacking boxes. Children are so good at recognizing significant moments, and they are able to live fully in the awe-inspiring present, relishing it with their total beings. Children are attentive to the mysteries of life, and if we let them, they bring these mysteries to our attention as well. And doing so, they restore our sense of wonder and awe.

In the interview I had with William, age twelve, I asked him if he thought he would have believed in God, even if no one had ever told him about God. He answered, "I think I would because

I would have wondered how things got here. There had to be a Creator. The things of nature are so beautiful and they bring us very close to God."

Children also help us learn again how to be dependent. Children are by nature dependent and are not ashamed of it. As adults, however, we put a great deal of value in being independent, and we strive diligently after that virtue. But one of the great lessons of the spiritual life is that we must learn to be dependent upon God. This is difficult for us, because we hate to give up our independence.

Jesus said, "Whoever does not receive the kingdom as a little child, shall not enter it." To become again as children is very hard to do. We think to do so is taking a step backwards. Children are quick to express their needs, often with very loud and very long voices. Have you ever heard a child say, "Come quick, Mama, I need you"? (The emphasis is most often on the "ne-e-e-d," drawn out as long as they can make it!) Or have you ever seen a child run to her or his father and crawl into his lap because they needed a hug or some reassurance? Children know their needs and are comfortable in expressing them. Our relationship to God should be like this too. We must give up trying to control our lives and learn to rely on God as a child relies on those significant adults in her or his life. This is the only way that God has space to do the work within us that is needed.

I have a friend who keeps a note posted on his computer. It says, "I have resigned as manager of the universe." When we learn to do this and put our dependence upon God, life takes on new meaning. A beautiful saying of one of our spiritual ancestors is this: "The day of my spiritual awakening was the day I saw and knew I saw all things in God and God in all things."[2] With this assurance, we can, with the confidence of the child, face all that life brings us. The psalmist says it so well.

But I have calmed and quieted my soul,
   like a weaned child with its mother;
   my soul is like the weaned child that is within me.
O Israel, hope in the LORD
   from this time on and forevermore.

Psalm 131: 2-3

We can learn from the child to calm and quieten our souls as we are held in the arms of a God who loves us and cares for us tenderly.

Children can teach us to trust God with the outcome of every situation in our lives. Our family took up camping some years ago, and although camping was not my favorite thing to do, I tried to join in good-naturedly.

On our first camping experience we were ambitious and drove into a deeply forested area in Colorado. Being novices at it, we had not planned well and arrived at the campsite almost at nightfall. Before we began setting up camp, the children wanted to explore the area. My husband, Tom, with the two boys and I with the two girls set out in opposite directions.

Suddenly, deep in the forest, it was almost as if someone had turned off all the lights. Night had descended upon us instantaneously, and I had never experienced such darkness. To make matters worse, a thunderstorm began and lightning was flashing everywhere. Immediately ahead of us, I could make out a small shed. We rushed to it, thankful for any kind of shelter.

The building had a tin roof, and the noise of the rain and loud claps of thunder, compounded by the lightning bolts cracking around us, were very frightening. I tried to appear as calm as possible, but in reality, I was terrified! As the noise and rain continued, Cindy, our oldest daughter, tugged on my arm. "It's all right, Mama," she said in a reassuring little voice, "Daddy will come for us soon." Not wanting to give any false hope, I said, "Well, honey, the thing is, Daddy doesn't know where we are." "That's all right," she again affirmed. "Daddy will find us. Daddy will come."

Not long afterwards, I saw the wobbly light of a flashlight coming through the woods towards us. Cindy saw it too and turned her little face toward me. "See," she said triumphantly, "I told you Daddy would come. I told you so." It was indeed Tom who had found our raincoats and an umbrella and had come to rescue us. As he gathered us under his arms and ushered us back to safety, I had to smile inwardly. Cindy's trust was unwavering.

This is the trust of children; and even in life's difficult circumstances, they keep that same faith in God. Children believe that God is able to do all that God says that God can do. In interviewing children, when I asked them what they prayed about, they always mentioned that they prayed to God when they had a problem or when they were troubled about something. They said they prayed especially for their families, and especially for their mothers and their fathers. Arkeita, age eight, said that she always prayed that God would "take care of my mama and daddy." Vatabia, age eight, answered with a touching comment when she said, "I pray that God will help the people in foster homes who do not have a home of their own." Montorias, age seven, said that he always prayed when he was afraid, asking God to take care of him. In every situation, the children stated that they believed that God had met their need, whatever it was.

My daughter Suzanne is a minister in a local church. In a previous appointment, during the times of intercessory prayer, her custom was to ask the congregation to name persons who were in need of prayer. No adult ever spoke aloud or mentioned a name. Consistently, however, Sunday after Sunday, a five-year-old boy raised his hand, and in a clear and confident voice, asked for prayer for someone who was ill or who had a problem. One Sunday he raised his hand and asked for prayers for the family of Dr. Seuss because he had seen on the television that Dr. Seuss had died! Nothing was beyond the strong arms of God for this child. Children are our guides in the area of trust and in the belief that prayers can be answered.

Children can give guidance in showing honor to the holy in our lives. Too often, for adults, things that are holy have become commonplace. We have seen it all and done it all, we think, and therefore meaningful moments of the holy go without recognition. Our eyes are dulled to the things of the spirit.

A minister tells the story of a young girl who was visiting the worship service with her aunt. When it came time for the communion service, the four year old listened intently as the pastor lifted the bread and said, "This is the bread of life offered for you." The girl turned to her aunt and exclaimed, "Aunt Deb, did you hear? The bread is for me! " The pastor continued, "The cup of salvation is offered for you for the forgiveness of sins." Again the child said, in a voice loud enough for all to hear, "Did you hear that, Aunt Deb? The cup is for me too." The minister then announced, "Please come to the table. Everything is ready." Even more excitedly, the little girl said, "Oh, look, Aunt Deb, look. The table is ready." The minister continued, "The table is for all. Please come, because the table is prepared for you." "Oh, Aunt Deb, look, look, the table is ready for me," the little girl exclaimed. Joyfully she approached the communion table, almost in disbelief that she had been invited to come.[3]

When we come to the communion table, do we come with the same awareness of the holy, a recognition that something special has been prepared for us? A holy moment is taking place at the communion table and too often we are so distracted that we do not recognize it. Children call us back to the holy, helping us to be conscious of the precious, present moment.

Children also help guide and mentor us in our spiritual life by reminding us to be spontaneous in our expression of joy. Children take delight in everything and see God's hand at work even in the ordinary things of life. Sometimes we adults get mired down in the ordinary. We become overloaded with cares and chores and confused priorities. Children cut through all of these and are able to respond spontaneously to whatever the present moment calls for.

Once when my daughter was saying the benediction following

the Sunday service at her church, her eyes focused upon a three-year-old child. Her parents had recently joined the church and the little girl was excited about coming every Sunday. Her parents had confided that they tried to come each Sunday because if they did not, the little girl would become upset.

As Suzanne began to pray, she noticed the little girl slip out of her pew and into the aisle. She stood there swaying back and forth during the prayer. As it concluded and the postlude began, the little girl raised her arms above her head and began to dance and turn, twirling round and round with the music. As the music stopped, she curtsied a small curtsy and stepped back into her pew, her dance finished.

For children, the ordinary or mundane becomes the edge of glory. Every moment holds for them the potential of being surprised by joy. How we need to be more spontaneous in our expressions of joy and thankfulness to God! We too need to take delight in everything and to see God in everything—even the ordinary things of life.

Children bring into our midst the very spirit of God. John Wesley has said that there are several known means of grace: That is, there are specific ways through which God comes to us. Some examples of these include prayer, fasting, and scripture reading. It is through these channels that we receive God's presence, God's grace. It seems to me that children also are a means of grace, for the spirit of God reveals itself to us through them.

The children I interviewed had a mysterious bond with God and were very open in sharing this connection. As I concluded the interview with Paige, age seven, I asked her if there was something additional that she wanted to share about God, something that I had not asked her.

Yes," she said, "there is. You know that I have figured something out."

"What is that, Paige?"

"Well, I have figured out that we are all adopted. All of our parents here on earth have adopted all of their children."

"How do you figure that?" I asked.

"Well, we are God's children first, and then when we come here to live with our parents, they have adopted us because we first belonged to God, our true parent."

"That's an interesting thought, Paige," I responded.

Wow, I thought, that is a very insightful concept. As children bring the spirit of God to us in so many ways, we wonder where these deep thoughts come from. And yet if we believe in the spirituality of the child, we know where they come from. A mysterious, awesome connnectedness exists between the child and God.

A story I heard recently powerfully illustrates how children bring the spirit of God into our midst. The event took place during the Special Oympics (the olympics for children with special needs). The children were lined up for a race to begin, some of them with braces on their legs, the rest with various other conditions. They were eager and ready to start. When the buzzer sounded, the children were off, ambling as best they could toward the finish line. Soon, one young boy took the lead and was obviously going to be the winner as he was far ahead of the others. Suddenly he stopped and looked around. When he did, he saw that one of the participants had fallen. Without thinking of his own victory, he turned around, went back and helped the boy to his feet. He put his arm around his friend, and together they started for the finish line. When the other contestants saw what he had done, they too stopped and went back, and with arms around one another, they all started for the finish line together. Surely this illustrates for us what the spirit of God in our midst can do.[4]

Finally, children bring us hope in the midst of all of life's situations. Woody Allen made the following statement at a commencement address. "More than any other time in history, [we] face a crossroads. One path leads to despair and utter hopelessness. The other, to total extinction. Let us pray we have the wisdom to choose correctly."[5]

We laugh at this statement and recognize that it was said in jest by a very funny man. Unfortunately, however, there are those who hold this pessimistic view about our personal, national, and world situations. Some persons have lost hope and live in a constant state of despair. When we see a child, full of joy and laughter, energy and optimism, hope surges within us, because a child is a symbol of the realm of God.

Some years ago, I saw a comic strip of a man and woman in their pajamas, drinking their coffee at the kitchen table. They had gloomy looks on their faces, and obviously their spirits were low. There is no color in the picture—it was drawn in black and white. In the next frame, their small child has entered the kitchen wearing footed pajamas and dragging his blanket behind him. This frame is in stark contrast to the first, because this one is in color. The sunlight is shining through the windows and the parents are smiling. The child has been the catalyst for change, and the entire situation has taken on a new dimension.

Several Christmases ago, I had gotten far behind with my Christmas preparations. Try as I might to maintain some perspective about it, I began to feel hurried and out of sorts. It was the week of Christmas, and I still needed to buy a gift for someone special.

Finally in desperation, I left the preparations I was involved in at home and went to the mall. It was filled with shoppers—many, many shoppers. Evidently I wasn't the only one who was trying to buy a gift at the last minute.

As I began to weave my way through the mall, people were bumping into each other with their packages, scowling at one another, and rushing madly from place to place. Suddenly a young mother came toward me with a child in a stroller. As they came near, I could hear the child singing softly at first and then as she continued down the mall, her voice grew louder and louder. Her words were familiar. She sang "Away in a Manger." She sang on and on, growing louder and louder. And it was as if a miracle had happened in the shopping mall. People slowed down, with smiles on their faces, to look at the child. Then they began smiling at one another, and as they continued on their way, their faces took on a different look. Their steps were lighter, their shoulders less tense, their demeanor less harried. Our day was changed because of the child. The innocent child in our midst brought to all of us a sense of joy and hope.

In some traditions when a baby is baptized, the people of faith sing the hymn "Child of Blessing, Child of Promise." One stanza includes this phrase "Fresh from God, refresh our spirits, into joy and laughter lead."[6]

Children are, indeed, spiritual guides and mentors for us. Evelyn Underhill says that "only the humble and childlike towards God, those who are receptive and have been long trained in lowliness, can be trusted to teach or show others the truth about God."[7] For this reason we need to listen to the words of children, to follow their example, to emulate their faith and trust, and to look with hope to the future. As Jesus has said, "Truly I tell you, whoever does not receive the kingdom of God as a little child will never enter it" (Mark 10: 15). When we do this, the peaceful vision that Isaiah tells us about, God's own vision, is attainable, because now it becomes possible for even a little child to lead us.

# CHAPTER NINE

# Guidance for Parents and Others Who Love Children

Dear God,

> Thank you for leting it rain for the florws. Please forgive me for evrything I've don. Please help the peopel that are sick. Please help the peopel that need food.

> Paige, age 8

*A*nother title for this chapter might be "Helpful Guidelines for Adults Who Are Beginning to Take Seriously Their Own Prayer Life, While at the Same Time Are Helping Children Learn to Pray." In these next few pages I hope to give some examples and techniques for your own prayer life as well as give encouragement to those who are helping their children learn to pray.

Perhaps you are just beginning a life of prayer and feel somewhat inadequate to try to guide a child in learning to pray. Or perhaps you have your own prayer life but don't know if you are capable of helping children with theirs. Do not feel overwhelmed! This responsibility is not so ominous as you might imagine. As I have said and will continue to say, the Holy Spirit is really the teacher and guide; you are just a gateopener who prepares a way for the Spirit to work.

First of all, when you are praying with children, remember that you don't have to use profound insights or large words. Pray simple prayers using language that children understand. This is all that is necessary. Begin with prayers of thanksgiving and gradually you will find that you and your child are capable of moving to other types of prayer.

If the child begins to ask some of the deep, difficult questions of life, as they often do, do not be reluctant to say that you don't know. Often the deepest questions of life have no specific answers, and it is completely appropriate to tell the child so. You can say, "I don't know the answer to that question, but we can work together to search for an answer." Much of life is mystery; a fact which children are quick to discover and understand.

John Westerhoff has said, "What our children are really asking is for us to reveal and share ourselves and our faith, not to provide dogmatic answers. We do not need to answer our children's questions, but we do need to make our faith available to them as a source for their learning and growth."[1] As children see you pray and as they observe your faith, they will be strengthened in their faith as well. The first concept we need to consider as busy parents, grandparents or other significant adults in the child's life is that of keeping our own lives centered in God. If we are to successfully communicate our faith and our belief in the power of prayer to our children, we must be growing in these areas ourselves. And in order to be growing in these areas, we must keep our own lives constantly centered in God.

We need to ask ourselves what it is that holds us fast when the trials and troubles, stresses and strains of life come to us? Do we have a center that calls us into the presence and power of God?

My oldest daughter, Cindy, is a potter. She makes beautiful vases and bowls and pots out of clay, and I am constantly amazed at all she creates. It is truly amazing to watch her take a glob of clay, put it on her potter's wheel, center and form the clay so that it eventually becomes a work of art.

She tells me that if the clay gets off center while she is making a pot, she must gently guide it back. It is impossible to make the object she desires if the clay is even a fraction off center. And if the pot or vase she is making loses its shape and does not turn out right, she just forms the clay into a ball again and reworks it. However, when it is centered and is formed by the skilled hands of an artist, wonderful creations are the result.

In the book of Jeremiah, we read these words:

> The word that came to Jeremiah from the LORD:
> Come, go down to the potter's house, and there I will let
> you hear my words. So I went down to the potter's house,

and there he was working at his wheel. The vessel he
was making was spoiled in the potter's hand, and he
reworked it into another vessel, as seemed good to him.
Then the word of the LORD came to me: Can I not do with
you, O house of Israel, just as this potter has done?
says the LORD. Just like the clay in the potter's hand,
so are you in my hand, O house of Israel.

Jeremiah 18:1-6

If we can keep centered in God's love, life takes on a totally different meaning. If we allow ourselves to get the slightest bit off
center, however, our lives become warped and misshapen. When
this happens, we then need the hands of God to guide us back to
the center and to rework us if necessary.

There are several ways that we can stay centered. We can pray
a breath prayer or the Jesus Prayer as a means of keeping centered. (See chapter 6 for details.) Or we might use various signals
throughout the day to call us into God's presence. If we are at
home and have a clock that chimes, we might use the chiming of
the hour as a reminder to keep ourselves centered in God.
Another way might be that every time we glance at our watch, we
can turn our hearts to God.

Other specific happenings can be a call to prayer for us such as
when the telephone rings, or when we are driving or see an ambulance, and so on. Frank Laubach has said that during the day we
all have "chinks of time" between doing the things that must be
done.[2] We can use these moments for times of prayer.

If we are working at the computer or cleaning or cooking or
doing work outside the home, we can stick notes with scripture or
other sayings in strategic places. When we see these notes, we are
called back to our center. The place for these notes should be
changed frequently because after a while, we grow accustomed to
seeing them and they no longer have any significance for us.
Carve out some space for yourself and God, right where you are,
whatever your life situation.

I have found it is very helpful to have a specific place for my longer time of prayer. It is wonderful to pray short prayers frequently, but we each need our specific place of prayer. This place will become sacred space if we use it frequently. Also having a certain time for our longer prayer time is beneficial because this helps to form the discipline of prayer in our lives. As we enter our space, perhaps we could light a candle and let this be our call to prayer.

A strengthening discipline is to pray short scripture verses or words of praise at the beginning of each day. Before getting out of bed, for example, say a part of the doxology such as "Praise God from whom all blessings flow." As you shower, use another verse regularly such as "I will bless the Lord at all times; his praise shall continually be in my mouth" (Psalm 34:1). As you dress use still another phrase such as "I will sing of your steadfast love, O LORD, forever; with my mouth I will proclaim your faithfulness to all generations" (Psalm 89:1). These words of praise and assurance set the tone for the day and place you and those you love in God's presence. The same process can be used in the evening as you prepare for bed.

In families today there are many crisis events: critical illnesses, problems at school for children, conflicts that seem to have no resolution, stresses that are job related, and fragmentation of the family circle. During times such as these, I have found that using an "anchor verse" gives me the strength I need. As I am reading the scripture, I try to do so formationally. That is, I don't read to gather information, but I try to discern what God is saying to me personally through the scripture that I am reading. Choosing a few short verses is better that trying to cover a large portion of scripture. Read the verses slowly and reflectively. Some people find it helpful to read the verses aloud. The chosen scripture should be used for an extended period of time, living with the words, meditating upon them, letting them slip into our subconscious.

If we read formationally, often a verse or a phrase will pop out at us. We may have read the passage many times before, but suddenly we see something new and fresh as if we were reading it for the first time. A passage will come alive that speaks directly to us. The part that does this can become, then, an anchor verse for us, steadying us in the storms of life. I like to write the chosen scripture on an index card and carry it in my purse when I go out, or put it in a window or on the mirror if at home. I can then refer to it many times a day, and before long, the verse or verses are committed to memory and become a part of me. These verses, I believe, are gifts from God to us and are able to strengthen and guide us in our daily lives.

During a time when two of our children were recuperating from lengthy illnesses we used the following passages.

So we do not lose heart. Even though our outer nature is wasting away, our inner nature is being renewed day by day. For this slight momentary affliction is preparing us for an eternal weight of glory beyond all measure, (or "glory beyond all comparison" in the RSV) because we look not at what can be seen but at what cannot be seen; for what can be seen is temporary, but what cannot be seen is eternal."

2 Corinthians 4:16-18

When my husband was having a difficult time following surgery, we used verses from Psalm 57:1-2.

Be merciful to me, O God, be merciful to me,
    for in you my soul takes refuge;
in the shadow of your wings I will take refuge,
    until the destroying storms pass by.

During a difficult time in my life when I was feeling overwhelmed and wondered if God had forgotten me, I prayed Psalm 103. To praise a good God, even when situations in our lives are not good, brings about a real attitude transformation.

> Bless the LORD, O my soul,
>     and all that is within me,
>         bless his holy name.
> Bless the LORD, O my soul,
>     and do not forget all his benefits —
> who forgives all your iniquity,
>     who heals all your diseases,
> who redeems your life from the Pit,
>     who crowns you with steadfast love and mercy,
> who satisfies you with good as long as you live
>     so that your youth is renewed like the eagle's.

As we read formationally, staying open to verses in the Bible that speak to our need, we will be amazed at how an appropriate and meaningful verse or verses catches our attention.

The discipline of keeping a journal can also enhance our prayer life. The ones I have kept over the years have been a way of keeping me centered in God's presence. As I journal, the words I write become a conversation between God and me. Remember that journaling differs from keeping a diary because in a diary, one relates the events of the day. In a journal, one reflects on life as seen in the presence of God. Some questions that we might reflect on as we write are "Where did I experience God today? What is God showing me in this event? What is God calling me to do in this situation?" In reading through old journals, I am constantly amazed at how the hand of God has led me and sustained me over the years. I think that you will find this discipline to be one that is very helpful in your spiritual journey as well.

There are times in our life of prayer when we feel that we are not getting anywhere, that our prayers have grown stale. During times like these, we must remember the passage from Romans 8:26-27.

> Likewise the Spirit helps us in our weakness;
>     for we do not know how to pray as we ought, but

that very Spirit intercedes with sighs too deep for
words. And God, who searches the heart, knows
what is the mind of the Spirit, because the
Spirit intercedes for the saints according to
to the will of God.

When we feel we do not know how to pray or when our faith is
weak, the Spirit is there to intercede for us. During these dry
times I have found that praying the prayers of others is a great
blessing. Make a collection of the prayers of some of the great
saints of the past or read prayers from a prayer book. This practice sustains and nourishes us until our own prayers begin to flow
again.

These then, are some prayer guidelines for you personally.


## WAYS TO PRAY FOR OUR CHILDREN

What a great legacy it is for our children to know that we are
praying for them! When we have doubts as to whether praying
for our children does any good, we can look at some strong examples from the past and the results speak for themselves.

For many years, as a young man, Augustine gave up on God
and lived a life of drunkenness and immorality. Monica, his
mother, never, however, gave up on him and continued to pray for
her son. She also asked others to pray for him. Finally, at age
thirty-one, Augustine became a Christian and went on to become
one of the early bishops of the church.

Catherine Booth was the wife of General William Booth of the
Salvation Army. Before her children were born, she promised
God that each one of them would be God's. She continued to pray
fervently for them throughout their lives and gave them a great
legacy of prayer. As a result, they have served faithfully in the Salvation Army throughout the years.

To be able to pray for and with our children is one of the greatest gifts that we can give them. I believe that our prayers for and with our children give to them a sense of rootedness in their lives. Children desperately need this if they are to find security and belonging in life. To pray for loved ones and friends, to talk about our faith, to lift the child to God in prayer all bring to the child a sense of connectedness with others and with God. Sometimes our faithfulness in prayer can ground our children until their faith has had time to develop deep enough roots.

There are no measurements or scales to measure how our prayers affect our children, but it is certain that there is power in our persistent prayer for and with our children. Because many persons throughout the ages have attested to this fact, we are given assurance that it is certainly worth the effort.

There are several specific ways to pray for and with children that I have found to be helpful. I call one "The Tucking-in Prayer." When my children were growing up, I would write a short, simple prayer on an index card. Then at bedtime we would pray the prayer together, and I would then slip the card under the child's pillow. This seemed to give them some sense of security and comfort. Once, one of our children drew beautiful pastel illustrations surrounding the prayer. I still have some of these tucked away.

Again, along these lines is the Pocket Prayer. On an index card — I keep the index card company in business, it seems! — or another small piece of paper, write short prayers, or scripture verses, or words of assurance. Put the card where the children will find it, perhaps in the child's pocket, lunch box, or book bag. They will be surprised and pleased to find them and to know that you are praying for them.

To pray in secret for our children strengthens both the child and the adult. Often as my children left for school and later for college, I would go to their rooms and kneel by their beds, remembering them to God in prayer. There is something special about being on our knees in prayer. Certainly we do not have to be on our knees every time we pray, but when we are in urgent prayer for our child, somehow being on our knees brings us closer to God.

If the child is having a problem, this is an especially good way to pray for her or him. I believe that the best way to pray for a child is in her or his room because you feel closer to the child when you are there. As I knelt by my child's bed, I would envision the one I was praying for in God's presence. I would see God's light and love surrounding the child, and imagine Jesus saying, "Let the children come." This type of prayer must be used often and for long periods of time. We must soak the child in God's love and light.

When praying like this, I tried not to dwell on the negative, whatever the problem was, but tried, instead, to envision the child whole and well and happy in every respect. Sometimes as parents, we focus too often on the negative, or the problem, instead of focusing on the positive results for which we are praying. When we dwell on the negative, these feelings seep into our subconscious, causing us to feel overwhelmed. Yet, when we focus on positive qualities, energy is released both in us and in our child.

We know from experience that our prayers for our children are not always answered immediately. But we must not give up praying for them. One of Jesus' most valuable teachings on prayer was about persistence in prayer. We must keep on praying, waiting upon the Lord who will answer our prayer whenever and however God chooses. In this day of instant gratification, we want answers to our prayers immediately. But God's ways are not our ways, therefore sometimes we must learn to wait, trusting in God's wisdom and power. This is not easy for any of us to do.

The Psalmist speaks of waiting on the Lord. "Our soul waits for the LORD; he is our help and shield" (Psalm 33:20).

Praying the scripture is another very helpful way to pray for our children, regardless of their age. In order to pray the scripture, we must read the Word meditatively and be open to the leading of the Holy Spirit. As you read, watch for some verse or passage that you feel reflects a situation in the life of the child for whom you are praying. Perhaps there is some joy in her or his life at the present moment for which you want to thank God. Perhaps he or she has some great need that is presenting a difficult problem and for which you feel an urgency to be in prayer.

After you have identified a passage, allow the words of the scripture to sink into your inner being as you read. And when a verse or passage comes alive for you, mark the verse, and begin praying the verse several times a day, envisioning God's love and light surrounding the child. I like to put the child's name and date by the verse or passage in my Bible so that it becomes a named place, a hallowed spot between the child and God.

Sometimes you may feel led to share the verse with the child so that you can pray the verse together; sometimes you will want the verse to remain between you and God. I have found that often I have waited for some time, even years, before sharing the verse with the child. For me, this type of prayer has been strengthening both for me and for the child for whom I am praying.

There are, of course, many other ways to pray for our children, but these are some that I have found helpful.

## RESOURCES THAT AID US IN OUR
## PRAYER PILGRIMAGE

We can strengthen our prayer life by reading some of the excellent books on prayer that are available. It takes a lifetime, actually, to learn to pray as we should and even in old age some of the saints of the past have confessed that they were just beginners in the spiritual life! Reading what others say about prayer can be helpful; however nothing can take the place of the actually praying. It is somewhat like swimming or riding a bicycle. You can read about it for years, but unless you get in the water or get on the bike, you will not learn how to swim or ride a bike.

Some books I have found helpful for those just beginning a prayer life are *Celebration of Discipline* and *Prayer: Finding the Heart's*

*True Home*, both by Richard Foster; *The Art of Personal Prayer* by Lance Webb; *The Workbook of Living Prayer*, by Maxie Dunnam; and *Beginning Prayer* by John Killinger.

For those who are farther along on their prayer journey you might add *A Guide to Prayer for All God's People* by Rueben Job and Norman Shawchuck and *The Way of the Heart* and *Life of the Beloved*, both by Henri Nouwen. These are just a few of the significant books on prayer available to us.

I would like to give a word of caution about books of prayers or books about prayer for children. This caution would apply to any book, but especially to books pertaining to God or prayer that we buy for our child to read. We should read the book first and ask ourself these questions. Is there anything in it that is contrary to the teachings of the Bible? Does it reflect the image of God that we want our child to have? Does it have a slant that is not compatible with our beliefs? Does it seem solid theologically? These same questions should be asked about the illustrations as well because pictures make an indelible impression on the child. There are so many books available and from so many sources, that we must use wisdom in our selections, carefully checking the wording and the concepts presented.

One example that presents concern is the prayer that we know as "Now I Lay Me down to Sleep." This has been used with children for years. However the phrase "if I should die before I wake, I pray Thee, Lord, my soul to take" is often troubling to children. This raises questions such as "Am I going to die tonight?" "Is God going to take me away?" Some of the more current versions of the prayer have changed the wording to "Thy love guard me through the night, And wake me with the morning light." This wording, I believe, is more appropriate for children.

I would mention, also, that there are many wonderful books, which, while not directly on spiritual subjects, can have a great impact on children's thinking. Some of these are *The Runaway Bunny* by Margaret Wise Brown, *Love You Forever* by Robert Munsch, and the books by Libba Moore Gray including *Miss*

*Tizzy* and *Dear Miss Willie Rudd*. These books are sound in their concepts and wording.

A beautiful series of books which are of a spiritual nature are the books for young children by Helen Caswell. The series is called "Growing in Faith Library" and include books such as *I Can Talk to God* and *Parable of the Leaven*. Millie S. Goodson has written a *Guide Book for Adults* to be used with this series and it is most helpful. The entire series would be a great addition to any child's library. As you select books for your child, select those appropriate for his or her age.


## PRAYER AS A LIFESTYLE

I would like to offer one final thought about children and prayer. Help children see that prayer time is important and a vital or natural part of their lives. Prayer must be woven into the fabric of their lives so that it is an integral part of the whole. A song which illustrates this point is "Teach me how to pray and teach me how to live. Make them one and the same to the glory of thy name."[3] As the words of the song illustrate, prayer can be a way of life for us.

Let us model our faith for our children. They should see us, not only in our private times of prayer, but when we are doing acts of mercy and kindness. They should learn that our prayer life forms who we are. We must take seriously Jesus' admonition to feed the hungry, to visit the sick and those in prisons and to share what we have with those less fortunate. Frank Laubach says, "prayer and action should be wedded."[4]

Whenever possible, children should be included in but not forced to be a part of these experiences. I remember one such incident in our family. Without letting the children take part in the decision making, Tom and I decided that one night a week we would have only soup and crackers for supper and donate the money that we would have spent to some worthy cause. Needless to say, this didn't go over well! There was much grumbling and complaining. We finally gave it up as a lost cause and learned a valuable lesson in the process.

Usually, however, deeds of kindness and service projects can be presented in such a way that children are eager to help. They take delight in making cookies for someone who is sick or picking flowers for a shut-in. Any experience like this reinforces in the child the strong values of kindness and goodness. By participating in them, children begin to realize that they can help God answer someone else's prayer.

Doing good deeds together, such as these mentioned, also will bring a closeness to the family. Studies of adolescent children have shown that family closeness fortifies children with an inner resistance to the toxins of life. The studies also show that children from close families are more likely to reject any kind of antisocial behavior. They are more likely to develop positive characteristics, such as adopting high moral standards, developing and keeping friends, embracing a religious faith, and involving themselves in helping others.[5]

Prayer time as a family is one powerful way to draw the family into a close relationship. As parents, grandparents, or other loved ones of children, our own consistent individual prayer times are also crucial as we endeavor to lead children into a life of prayer. The pilgrimage of prayer is a shared one with our children, but in order for us to provide guidance for them, we must be growing in our own life of prayer.

## CONCLUSION

John Wesley has stated that we should set aside some part of every day for private devotions: What may seem hard to do at first will even, after a time, become something that you look forward to doing. Give your soul time and space to grow, Wesley exhorted.[6] And begin now to teach the child or children in your life, not just about prayer, but actually how to pray. It is never too early to begin, nor is it too late, regardless of the age of the children. As you travel on this spiritual quest together, you will learn many valuable lessons of faith from each other.

In the Judeo-Christian tradition, we are people who have taken very seriously the commandment to teach our children about God. Beginning long ago with Moses, as he brought the children of Israel out of slavery in Egypt and into the Promised Land, the commandment was clear. He told the Israelites that they were to keep the story of who they were and what God had done for them alive by telling and retelling it to their children. Lest they should forget, they were to diligently instruct their children in the commandments and promises of God. Moses tells them specifically how to do this:

> You shall put these words of mine in your heart and soul, and you shall bind them as a sign on your hand, and fix them as an emblem on your forehead. Teach them to your children, talking about them when you are at home and when you are away, when you lie down and when you rise. Write them on the doorposts of your house and on your gates, so that your days and the days of your children may be multiplied in the land that the LORD swore to your ancestors to give them as long as the heavens are above the earth.
>
> Deuteronomy 11:18-21

We, as the covenant people of God, are given this same commandment today. God is calling us to do for our children what God, through Moses, mandated the Israelites to do so long ago. We are to teach our children about God and the things of God, talking about them when we are at home and when we are away, and when we lie down and when we rise.

One important difference between us, however is this: Whereas Moses and the children of Israel were people of the Old

Covenant, we, as the Christian community, are the people of the New Covenant. Jesus was sent by God as the sign of the New Covenant with his people, assuring us that we are, indeed the beloved daughters and sons of God. Jesus brought us the New Commandants: love of God and love of neighbor as ourselves. We, as the people of the New Covenant, have therefore, our own stories to tell, just as the people of the Old Covenant had their stories to tell. We can tell how God has brought us out, like the Israelites of old, from the desert places of our lives into new and fresh and fertile life-giving oases. Because of who we are, our children need to hear the stories of how God has been faithful in our lives throughout all our wanderings and that, because of Jesus, we are a redeemed and forgiven people. They need to see us modeling with our lives the faith we proclaim with our lips. They need to learn the commandments and promises of God that give our lives structure and meaning. They need to know that the God who created us longs to be in relationship with us and that prayer is the language that keeps us connected to our Maker.

We must be bold in teaching our children about God because the world is bold in what it is teaching our children.[7] This can be no halfhearted attempt on our part because the stakes are too high. Moses told the people of the Old Covenant, "Take care, or you will be seduced into turning away, serving other gods and worshiping them" (Deuteronomy 11:16). That danger is very real for us today. Only in teaching our children who God is will they come to know fully who they are. Their identity is hidden within the God who has created them and who loves them with an unconditional, everlasting, and passionate love, and wants to be in a loving relationship with them.

Jesus has said, "Truly I tell you, just as you did it to one of the least of these who are members of my family, you did it to me" (Matthew 5:40). Our children are indeed among "the least of these" in our society today. We, as Christian adults, have a solemn responsibility to protect and guide and train these young ones who are in our care. Perhaps they may be among "the least," but they are, nonetheless, according to Jesus, the ideal members of the kingdom of God.

Lest these children who are in our care forget the "original vision"—that mysterious bonding between themselves and God that once was theirs when they arrived from heaven— we need to tell them our stories, nurture them in the faith, teach them the commandments and promises from the Holy Scripture, and lead them into a life of faithfulness in prayer. We do this with the assurance that if we act as gateopeners for the Holy Spirit, the Holy Spirit will come and guide us in this pilgrimage. May God give to each one of us the desire, the wisdom, the strength, and the courage to begin praying with and for our children—and to begin now.

# *Interviews with Children*

I am extremely grateful to the children who agreed to be interviewed. They were so sincere in their answers and their spontaneous responses were from their hearts. I did not sense in any way that they were trying to give the answers that they thought I expected or wanted but truly answered according to their own feelings and experiences. To ask children to reveal the deepest thoughts of their hearts is an awesome request and I am aware of my responsibility to use their answers in a trustworthy manner. Therefore, as I share these interviews with you, I ask that you read them reverently and treat them with the utmost respect, knowing that an innocent child has shared his or her innermost thoughts with you. These interviews include children from Euroamerican, African American and Native American cultures. They include children from affluent families as well as children from lower income families. In addition to individual children who have talked with me, I am grateful to the children of Belle Meade United Methodist Church, Nashville, Tenessee; Davis Street United Methodist Church, Burlington, North Carolina; Hitchitee United Methodist Church, near Seminole, Oklahoma; and Nancy Webb Kelly United Methodist Church,

Nashville, Tennessee. My life has been immeasurably enriched by my encounters with these precious children.

Rachel was a very alert, verbal five year old. She was very willing to answer my questions and seemed at ease with our conversation. We met at a local restaurant and drank a soft drink as we talked. I explained to her that I was meeting with various children and talking with them about God and about prayer. I assured her that there were no right or wrong answers to the questions, but that I just wanted to know her own feelings about the questions I asked. I used this same procedure with all the children I interviewed. Following is the interview with Rachel.

B:   Rachel, do you remember the first time that you ever prayed?

R:   (After thinking about the question a while) Oh, yes, I remember. I think that it was when I was first born. I talked to God right then, when I was born.

B:   And now, at the age you are now, when do you pray now?

R:   I pray before I eat and before I go to bed.

B:   And what do you pray about?

R:   Well, I pray about a lot of things. I ask God to bless my Mama, Daddy, and sister. And I ask God to take care of my Grandpa and Nana. And I ask God to bless Ma. (Here she paused, thinking a minute before continuing.) My other grandfather died when I was two years old, but I got to go see him in the hospital before he died. (She seemed pleased that she saw him before he died.)

B:   If you want something really bad, Rachel, like a toy or a bike or something, do you ask God for those kinds of things?

R:  No, I don't ask God for those kinds of things. I just tell my Mama and Daddy and they get them for me on my birthday or some other time.

B:  Do you remember a time when God was very close to you—when you felt that God was right there with you?

R:  (Thinking a minute and then laughing out loud) Yes! I remember. It was on my birthday when I was having a lot of fun.

B:  Are there other times when you feel close to God and know that God is close to you?

R:  Yes. When I am out in my backyard. There are some big bushes and weeds and sometimes when I am out there by myself, I feel afraid. God takes care of me. But my dog and cat protect me too!

B:  Are there any other times when you feel that God is close to you?

R:  Yes, when I am sad sometimes.

B:  Rachel, if there were some girls in your school who didn't know God, didn't even know who God was, how would you describe God to them?

R:  Well, I would just say, "Both of you come over here and I will tell you about God. God is very special. He is all around you even though you don't know it. God protects you and heals you too when you are sick."

B:  If I asked you to draw a picture of God, could you do that? What would you draw God to look like?

R:  (Here she laughs and laughs with her hand over her mouth.) Oh, I couldn't draw a picture of God because I don't really know what God looks like. I think that God has a beard and a mustache, though.

B:  What stories from the Bible help you to know what God is like?

R:  Well, I like the story about when there was a big storm and God made the water be still. (Thinking again) And, uh, I like the story of the Good Samaritan. That's my favorite story.

B:  What are some of the prayers you say to God?

R:  Well, I thank God for the trees and flowers and I thank God for the food. And at night, I say "Now I lay me down to sleep."

B:  If I asked you to tell me who is closer to God than anyone else, who would you say?

R:  Why, I would say Pa, because Pa has gone to live with God and Jesus. And then my aunt's baby is close to God because he died when he was born.

B:  Do you think that it is easier to pray to God when it is quiet or when it is noisy?

R:  Oh, when it is quiet, that's for sure. All that noise keeps me from hearing God.

B:  Is it easier to pray when you are by yourself or when you are with someone?

R:  Well, sometimes I like to pray by myself, and then sometimes I like to pray with Mom.

B:  Do you believe in angels, Rachel? Have you ever seen an angel?

R:  Well, I know that there are angels, but the only ones I have seen are some in a store. (I didn't pursue this issue.)

B:  Is there anything else you would like to say about God that I haven't asked you about?

R:  Well, I would like to tell people that God knows what is best for them, and we need to trust God. And that God is kind and is never, never mean.

The following interview is with Grace, who is nine years old and is in the fourth grade. Grace belongs to the Roman Catholic tradition.

B:   Tell me, Grace, can you remember the first time you ever prayed?

G:   Well, I don't remember exactly, but I think it was when I was in church and when I was very young.

B:   When are the times that you pray now?

G:   I pray before I go to sleep, and I pray during the daytime at church and sometimes at school.

B:   What are the things that you pray about?

G:   I pray about other people. I ask God to take care of my mom and me and my brother.

B:   When is God the closest to you? When do you feel God is near you?

G:   God is closest to me at night. I know God is there for sure.

B:   If I asked you to draw a picture of God, what do you think God looks like? How would you draw God?

G:   God is like a parent—maybe either a mother or a father. God helps you through all of your troubles and is very nice. I think that God is very big and talks very loud.

B:   What stories from the Bible help you to know about God?

G:   Well, I know more stories about Jesus than I do about God. My favorite story about Jesus is the story of the cross.

B:   Can you remember a time that you prayed and you felt that God answered your prayer?

G:   When I am afraid and really, really scared I say the Guardian Angel Prayer and then I'm not scared any more.

B:   Could you say the Guardian Angel Prayer for me? I'm not sure that I know it.

G:   Sure, it goes: Guardian angel, protector dear. To whom

God's love commits me here. Ever this night be at my side
To light, to guard, to rule, to guide.

B: That's a beautiful prayer, Grace. Who taught it to you?

G: My mom did.

B: Grace, who do you know that is closer to God than anyone else?

G: Well, I would have to say my mom or the priest at church.

B: Do you think that it is easier to pray when it is quiet or when it is noisy?

G: Definitely when it is quiet. Noise keeps you from thinking about God.

B: Do you like to pray by yourself or with someone else?

G: Sometimes I like to pray by myself and sometimes with other people, especially my mom.

B: Do you always use prayers that you have memorized like the Guardian Angel prayer, or do you sometimes just say whatever you want to.

G: I sometimes say memorized prayers like the Guardian Angel Prayer and the Our Father, but then sometimes I just say whatever I am thinking in my heart.

Allison was the youngest child I interviewed. She was three years old and had an older brother and sister. She was very much at ease and seemed not to mind answering my questions.

B: Allison, when did you first pray to God? Do you remember?

A: I don't know. I guess it was either at home or at church.

B: When do you pray now?

A: I pray at night time and sometimes I pray at school.

B: What do you pray about?

A: I say, "Thank you God for friends who love us and for helping us grow." I sometimes pray, "Our father who art in heaven."

B: What else do you say to God?

A: Well, I say, "I love you."

B: And does God say anything to you in return?

A: Yes, God says, "I love you too, Allison!" (Here she giggles.)

B: Have you ever seen heaven?

A: Not yet, but I will when I die.

B: If you drew a picture of God, what would God look like? How would you draw God?

A: I would draw a lot of circles on the page and color it pink all over.

B  Do you think that it is easier to pray when it is quiet or when it is noisy?

A: When it's quiet. You can pray better then and hear God better.

Paige is seven years old and has an older brother. She is very articulate and seemed to have a good time during the interview. These are the questions I asked Paige.

B: When was the first time you can remember praying, Paige?

P. It was when I was three years old.

B: What did you pray for then?

P. I prayed that everyone would be okay.

B: And when do you pray now?

P. I pray in the mornings and night—especially at bedtime. Sometimes I pray in the afternoons too if I have troubles.

B: Can you remember a time when you felt closest to God?

P.     Yes, I can remember. It was when I was itty, bitty. I just felt like I was hugging God. (She paused a minute as if thinking.) You know, I can just barely remember when I was in heaven.

B:     Could you describe God or tell what God is like to someone who doesn't know?

P.     Why I would tell them that God made them and loves them and wants to be with them.

B:     Do you have any idea what God looks like?

P.     I'm not for sure, but I think he has a beard that is blackish or brownish and that he wears a white and blue robe.

B:     Do you think it is better to pray when you are by yourself or with others?

P.     I think it is better to pray when you are by yourself.

B:     Do you think it is better to pray when it is quiet or when it is noisy?

P.     It is better to pray when it is quiet. I can't pray when the TV is going and there is all that crunching on potato chips and stuff. (Here she laughs.)

B:     Is there anything else you would like to tell me about God and prayer that I haven't asked?

P.     (She pauses to think about something.) Well, yes. I have been thinking about something lately. You know, don't you, that we are all adopted by our parents, because we are all God's children first and then God lets us come to live with our parents. So we are all adopted!

Parker, age twelve, was Paige's brother. He also was articulate and was very willing to answer my questions.

B:     Parker, do you remember the first time that you knew there was a God?

P:  Well, I remember that in the first grade my teacher brought this experience to me. Maybe I had known this earlier, but I remember this time very well. She asked us to pray and to open the door of our hearts so that God could come in.

B:  I'm glad that you remember that. Do you remember a time when you felt that God was closer to you than any other time that you can identify?

P:  Whenever I'm in trouble, I know that God is close to me. I don't mean just physical trouble, but other times too like during mental trouble and times when I am stressed out during exams.

B:  What do you think God is like, Parker?

P:  Well, I think God is strict, but also forgiving. I think of God in human form because He made Adam. Maybe I think of God as an old man with a long and flowing gray beard and gray hair. God may be old, but he is still very strong and very wise.

B:  If you were trying to tell someone about God, someone who had never heard about God, what would you say?

P:  Well, I would say that God is almost like a "fall back." God is there to save you when you fail or fall. He gets you out of trouble. God is a friend, someone you can turn to in good or bad situations.

B:  That is well said, Parker. If someone wanted you to draw a picture of God, what would you draw?

P:  I don't know if you have seen "The Christmas Carol" and the ghost of Christmas past. But the ghost flickers and well, it's almost too much to imagine. God is like that. There is an aura around God—a light. God may have two legs and two arms one minute, but then they might become twenty arms or legs. God ages, I think, and looks like you need him to look for the situation you are in.

B:  That's an interesting concept, Parker. Who is someone who is closer to God than anyone you know?

P:   Missionaries seem to be very much in touch with God. (Parker had gone with his youth group on a mission trip during the summer to repair and paint a Native American church.)

B:   I think you are right about that. Tell me, Parker, do you remember the first time that you ever prayed?

P:   Well, when it was on my own, I guess it was in the first grade. I'm sure that I prayed before that though.

B:   When do you pray now?

P:   For serious prayer, I pray fifteen minutes or so at night. But I also pray before meals, asking God to bless the food. I also pray at church and at church-related events and I pray to God when I am in troubled situations.

B:   What are the things that you pray about?

P:   I pray about a lot of things. To begin, I pray for protection for my family. I pray for forgiveness and ask God to help me forgive those people that I need to forgive. When I am falling asleep, I try to have pure thoughts and offer prayers of thanksgiving to God. Then I end with the Lord's Prayer.

B:   That sounds like a good plan. What stories from the Bible have helped you know what God is like?

P:   Well, I don't know. Different situations call for different stories.

B:   Parker, do you think it is easier to pray when it is quiet or when it is noisy?

P:   When it is quiet because I can concentrate better.

B:   Do you find it easier to pray when you are by yourself or when you are with someone else?

P:   I can pray with others, but I think I pray better by myself.

B:   Do you believe in angels, Parker?

P:   Yes, I believe in angels, but I have never seen one.

Barry was very shy and a bit hesitant to answer my questions at first. He became more vocal as the interview progressed. Barry was nine years old and had two sisters and one brother.

BE:  Hi, Barry. I would like to ask you some questions about God and about prayer. Would that be all right with you?

BA:  Sure.

BE:  Well, I would like for you to think a minute. Do you remember the first time that you knew there was a God?

BA:  Yes, I remember. It was one day when I was very little.

BE:  Do you remember a time when you felt God has been close to you?

BA:  Sure, every time that I am going to sleep.

BE:  What do you think that God is like, Barry?

BA:  He is like a father. He is kind and nice.

BE:  If you were trying to tell someone about God, someone who had never heard about God before, what would you say?

BA:  Well, I would just say that God lives in the sky and that he's nice and he helps us.

BE:  If someone wanted you to draw a picture of God, what would you draw?

BA:  (Barry laughs) Why, I would just draw God! He would have a white robe on and have blue eyes and blond hair. I don't think that he would have a beard, though.

BE:  Who is someone closer to God than anyone you know, Barry? By that I mean someone who lives like God wants us to live and stays in touch with God.

BA:  My mama. She goes to church every week and prays every night with me.

BE:  That's good, Barry. Do you remember the first time that you ever prayed?

BA:  Yes, when I was three I prayed all by myself.

BE:  When do you pray now?

BA:  Before going to sleep, when I wake up, and when I eat. I also pray at school when I get worried about something.

BE:  What are the things that you pray about?

BA:  I pray for my family, for God to take care of them. I pray for some people who are old or very sick.

BE:  That's good, Barry. What stories from the Bible help you know what God is like?

BA:  Matthew 1:12.

BE:  And what story does it tell in Matthew 1:12?

BA:  It's the story of the man who was mean and Jesus punished him and then he got his act back together. (I was not sure exactly what story Barry was talking about! When I tried to question him further, he didn't want to say anymore about it.)

BE:  Barry, do you think that it is easier to pray when it's quiet or when it is noisy?

BA:  When it is quiet. If there is a whole lot of noise, I can't pray.

BE:  Do you think that it is easier to pray with someone or when you are by yourself?

BA:  With somebody, but I can pray by myself too.

BE:  Do you believe in angels, Barry?

BA:  Yes.

BE:  Have you ever seen one?

BA:  Just on television. I saw a movie once called "Angels in the Outfield" and in it, a boy prayed for angels to come and help his dad's team win the ball game and they won.

Robert was nine years old. He told me that he had on older brother and two sisters, ages eleven and thirteen.

B:  Do you remember the first time that you knew that there was a God, Robert?

R:  Yes, I remember. I saw this big yellow sun and it reminded me of God. At first, I thought it was God, and then I saw it was the sun that God had created.

B:  What do you think God is like?

R:  Why, he is like a big person.

B:  If you were trying to tell someone about God, someone who had never heard about God, what would you say?

R:  I would say that he is "the Man Upstairs." He is the one who always helps us, just like my daddy and my uncle.

B:  If someone wanted you to draw a picture of God, what would you draw?

R:  Why I would just draw the real God! He would have white clothes on with a little bit of blue and he would have black hair and blue eyes.

B:  Who is someone closer to God than anyone you know?

R:  Why Jesus is. Also my mama because she is so good to me.

B:  Do you remember the first time that you ever prayed to God?

R:  Yes, I remember. It was when I was in bed and I was about six years old.

B:  When do you pray now?

R:  I have been praying all this week. I kneel down and pray by myself.

B:  What are the things that you pray about?

R:  I pray about a lot of things. I pray about my family and I wish my daddy would come back alive. I pray for the sick to get well.

B:  What stories from the Bible help you know what God is like?

R:    I can't remember right now.

B:    That's okay. Maybe you will remember some later. Let me ask you this: Is it easier to pray when it is quiet or when it is noisy?

R:    When it is quiet, cause when there is a lot of noise, I keep messing up.

B:    Is it easier to pray when you are by yourself or when you are with someone?

R:    By myself.

B:    Do you believe in angels?

R:    No. (After he thinks a little while he responds again.) Well, I mean, well, sure, but I have never seen an angel except on TV.

Scott was eight years old and in the second grade. He was very open to my questions and answered them without hesitation.

B:    Hi, Scott. You remember I asked you if you would be willing to talk to me and to answer some questions?

S:    Yes, I remember.

B:    Well, thanks for doing this. This is the first question that I would like for you to think about. Do you remember the first time you knew that there was a God?

S:    Well, I'm not sure what age I was. Maybe five or so. My dad put it into words that I could understand. Maybe I knew it before then, though.

B:    What do you think God is like, Scott?

S:    Why God is great! God is perfect. In fact God is unbelievable!

B:    If you were trying to tell someone about God, someone who had not heard about God, what would you say?

S:    I would probably tell them about God and how he sent

Jesus to save us. I would invite them to church with me and hopefully they would learn who God is.

B: If someone wanted you to draw a picture of God, what would you draw?

S: Oh man! (smiling) That's hard! Jesus was a man, and God made man in his own image so we must look like God.

B: Who is someone closer to God than anyone you know?

S: Well, I know people who are at least trying to live close to God. My parents especially are trying to live close to God.

B: Do you remember the first time that you ever prayed?

S: Maybe when I was a year or two old I learned to bow my head. I'm sure that I saw someone pray when I was first born and then I began to pray myself.

B: When do you pray now?

S: I pray a lot during the day when I need help. I pray when I go to bed and at meal times. In the morning, I read my Bible and have a prayer then.

B: What are the things that you pray about?

S: I pray that I will have a good day. I thank God for all that I have. I pray for our friend in Africa, and for all my friends and family here.

B: What stories from the Bible help you know what God is like?

S: Well, the stories that tell the things that Jesus did. How he gave up his life so that we can live.

B: Do you think that it is easier to pray when it is quiet or when it is noisy?

S: When it is quiet. I can think better and communicate better with God then. We can still pray when it is noisy but it takes more concentration.

B: Is it easier to pray when you are by yourself or with someone?

S: By myself. But I guess it depends on who I am with.

B:    Do you believe in angels?

S:    Yes. Sometimes I know that they are there, but I have never seen one myself.

Shameka was eight years old and in the second grade. She was very open and happy and eager to talk.

B:    Shameka, do you remember the first time that you knew that there was a God?

S:    Yes, I do remember. I have always been thinking about God. In fact, I was just thinking about God now.

B:    Do you remember a time when God was closer to you than any other time?

S:    Yes, I was dreaming in my bed one night and I thought God was right there with me. It seemed to me like he was.

B:    What is God like?

S:    God is a spirit.

B:    If you were trying to tell someone about God, someone who had never heard abut God, what would you say?

S:    I would say that God is a special person to everyone. God helped my grandmother once to not be hit by a truck when she was crossing the street. He protects me when I walk to school every day.

B:    If someone asked you to draw a picture of God, what would you draw?

S:    Why I'd just draw God! God would be big and have on "regular clothes." He would have brown hair and blue eyes and he would be up in heaven.

B:    Who is someone closer to God than anyone you know?

S:    Martin Luther King, Jr.

B:    Do you remember the first time that you ever prayed?

S:  Yes, when I was two years old and I was with my daddy.

B:  When do you pray now?

S:  I say grace before meals three times a day, and I say prayers at night. I pray in church and when we leave for church. I pray when I take a nap, and I pray at school when I have a problem.

B:  What are the things that you pray about?

S:  I pray about—well, I thank God who created everything on earth and all the animals. My daddy said not to be asking God for money, so I don't do that. I pray for the sick people and I ask God to take care of my family.

B:  What stories from the Bible help you know what God is like?

S:  I can't think right now.

B:  That's okay. Maybe you will remember later. Tell me, Is it easier to pray when it is quiet or noisy?

S:  When it's quiet. You can hear the spirit of God better when it's quiet.

B:  Is it easier to pray when you are by yourself or with someone?

S:  It's kinda easier to pray when you are by yourself because it is quieter then and you can think better.

Jamie was thirteen and was very shy. She answered my questions in very short answers. She was pleasant but was hesitant to share very much.

B:  Jamie, do you go to church?

J:  Yes, I go to this church (Hitchitee United Methodist Church).

B:  Do you remember when you first prayed?

J:   Yes, I remember. It was at a church camp a few years ago.

B:   When do you pray now?

J:   I pray sometimes when I am worried or scared. I pray sometimes when we eat.

B:   Who was the first person that you ever heard pray?

J:   It was a preacher. That was the first person that I heard pray.

B:   Who do you think is closer to God than anyone you know?

J:   Well, I would have to say my grandpa and the minister at the church. My grandpa helps me a lot, like one time when I messed up, he told me that God would forgive me for what I did. That made me feel better.

B:   What do you think that God looks like, Jamie?

J:   Well, I think that he is tall and wears a white gown. He has a brown beard and brown hair.

B:   Is there anything that you would like to talk about that we haven't talked about?

J:   Well, yes. There is something I've always wanted to know. How long does a guardian angel stay with you? Where do they go when you die?

B:   Those are good questions, Jamie. What do you think?

J:   Well, I don't know. Maybe when you die, your guardian angel goes and becomes the guardian angel for someone else.

B:   That's a good thought, Jamie. I guess that we really don't know the answers to your questions. I'm not sure that anyone does.

The following are excerpts from the interviews with John, William, Paty, and Clint, who are all twelve.

Interview with John

B:  John, do you remember when you first said a prayer?

J:  Well, I think it was when I was very young and my dad tucked me in at night. We probably started with praying "Now I lay me down to sleep" and then I added other prayers as I got older.

B:  Do you think it is easier to pray by yourself or with someone else?

J:  I think it is easier to pray silently by myself. We have a moment of silence at my school and I use that time for prayer.

B:  Is there a time God has answered your prayers in a special way?

J:  Yes, there was a time. When my parents were getting a divorce, I was very sad and I prayed a lot. God helped me a lot during that time.

B:  What do you think that God is like, John?

J:  Well, I think that we are lucky to have a God like we have. God is a forgiving God. I picture him as a man, maybe a king, with a beard and a mist all around him. I know that God is more than a man, though.

Interview with William

B:  William, do you remember the first time that you ever prayed?

W:  It probably was at church, but I really don't remember because it was so long ago.

B:  What are the things that you pray about now?

W:  Well, I pray for my family and for people who are sick or who are in trouble. I also pray in bad situations when I need help. An example might be when I was running in a cross country race recently and needed strength. I prayed about that.

B:   Do you know when it was that you first believed in God?

W:   I think that must have been when I was about eleven. I had always been told about God, but I came to know it myself at age eleven.

B:   Do you think you would have believed in God even if no one had ever told you about God?

W:   Yes, I think I would have, because I would have wondered how things got here—about who created things. I think that nature brings you closer to God. I think that in all the wonderful things of nature we can find God.

Interview with Paty

B:   Paty, can you remember the first time that you ever prayed?

P:   No, I don't think that I can remember. It was so long ago.

B:   What are the things that you pray about now?

P:   I pray for my family, and I give thanks for having food to eat and for having a nice home and friends and relatives.

B:   Do you remember when God has been closer to you than any other time?

P:   Yes, I remember. When my grandfather died, we were very sad. I felt a real sense of God's presence with us then.

Interview with Clint

B:   Clint, do you remember the first time that you ever prayed?

C:   I would say that it was probably at church. It was so long ago that I just can't remember.

B:   When do you pray now, Clint?

C:   I pray mostly at night, but I pray other times too.

B:   What are some things that you pray about?

C:   I pray for my family and friends. I thank God for shelter, food, and clothes. I say "thanks" for all that God has done. Sometimes I just say "help" when I need God.

B:   Do you remember a special time when you thought that God was very close to you?

C:   Yes, I remember one night when I was in bed and I thought God was very close. I was just lying there and everything was very quiet and I could feel God's presence with me.

Excerpts from interviews with Katie, Ellie, and Jessica, all twelve years old.

Interview with Katie

B:   Katie, if you were describing God to someone who did not know God, how would you describe God?

K:   Well, I would describe God as a creator, or a father, someone you can trust and put faith in. It doesn't matter what race you belong to or what church you go to, we have the same God.

B:   What do you think God looks like?

K:   That's hard to say. He might have on a shiny robe, but no face. I couldn't describe God's face because we just don't know what he looks like.

B:   Who is a person that you feel is more like God or is closer to God than anyone you know?

K:   Well, I do know someone like that. This man in our church (she gives his name) is so kind to my brother. He shows the attributes of God.

B:   What are the things that you pray about, Katie?

K:   I pray differently now than I did when I was four years old. Then I asked for things. Now I ask God to be with me and my family and things like that.

Interview with Ellie

B:   Ellie, could you tell me what you think God is like?

E:   I think God is very forgiving and is always there for you. I am amazed that when I pray, there might be millions of other people praying at the same time. It is hard to understand how God can listen and answer so many prayers!

B:   If you were trying to tell someone about God, someone who had never heard about God, what would you say?

E:   I would just say that God is always there for you. God will forgive you and will give you many, many chances to make things right.

B:   If someone wanted you to draw a picture of God, what would you draw?

E:   Well, there are so many ways that we can describe God. We get many images of God from the Bible. We could describe God as the Alpha and the Omega, or as a Rock or as a Burning Bush.

B:   Ellie, do you believe in angels?

E:   Yes, definitely. Everyone has a guardian angel that watches over them day and night. Your favorite angel or your guardian angel might come to you at night and reveal what their name is.

Interview with Jessica

B:   Jessica, could you tell me when you first prayed?

J:   Well, that's hard to remember. Probably at church or at home with my family at night when we're going to bed.

B:   What are the things that you pray about now?

J:   My family, for God to guide us in the right way and I ask God to take care of us.

B:  Can you think of a time when God answered your prayers in a very real way?

J:  Yes, I can. I have been having trouble with my back and we didn't know what it was. I have been praying about it and God has answered my prayers. I have had testing done on my back and the doctors now know what the problem is. I will have surgery soon to correct the problem.

B:  Can you think of a time when you felt God's presence very close to you?

J:  Yes. When my grandfather died and we were at the cemetery, I felt God very close to all of us.

Excerpts from various interviews.

Rachel H., age ten

B:  Rachel, if someone wanted you to draw a picture of God, how would you draw God?

R:  I would probably draw God to look like an angel. He would have a brown beard and green eyes and wear a white robe.

B:  What do you think heaven is like, Rachel?

R:  Heaven is a place where everyone loves one another. I know a lot of people who will be there. Many of the people in the Bible will be there, that's for sure.

Courtney, age five

B:  If you were trying to tell someone about God, someone who had never heard about God, what would you say?

C:  Well, I would sing them a song about God. And I would tell them that God loves me and that God loves them too.

Vatabia, age eight

B:    Do you remember a time when God was very close to you?

V:    Yes, when I was born, God was right there. Another time was when I heard the pretty music in our church on Christmas, God was there too.

B:    What are some of the things that you pray about?

V:    I pray about everything. I ask God to help people in the foster homes who do not have a home. I pray and ask God to take care of them and make them okay.

Brenda, age nine

BE:  Brenda, if someone wanted you to draw a picture of God, what would you draw?

BR: I would draw God like a spirit rising up in the air. He would have a face, but I don't know what kind; and he would have gray hair and would be wearing a white robe with a cross on it.

BE:  What stories from the Bible help you know what God is like?

BR:  The verse "In the beginning God created the heaven and the earth" tells me about God.

Arkeita, age eight

B:    Arkeita, do you remember the first time that you knew that there was a God?

A:    Yes. My mama told me about God. How God made us and all.

B:    If you were trying to tell someone about God, someone who had never heard about God, what would you say?

A:    I would say that God is in our country and God is in our hearts and God helps us. God is with us when we go somewhere on a trip or when we move away. God will be right there with us.

Lana, age eight

B:     Lana, did you ever see anything that reminded you of God?

L:     Yes, I saw a rainbow once and it was beautiful and it made me think of God.

B:     Who is a person closer to God than anyone that you know?

L:     My uncle is because he prays and goes to church a lot.

# Prayers

Let the words of my mouth,
and the meditation of my heart,
be acceptable in thy sight, O LORD,
my strength, and my redeemer.

> *Psalm 19:14, King James Version*

Lord, teach me all that I should know;
In grace and wisdom I may grow;
The more I learn to do Thy will,
The better may I love Thee still.

> Isaac Watts
> A *Child's Book of Prayers*, p. 2

Dear Father, hear and bless
Thy beasts and singing birds,
And guard with tenderness
Small things that have no words.

> Anonymous
> A *Child's Book of Prayers*, p. 3

God be in my head,
 And in my understanding;
God be in my eyes,
 And in my looking;
God be in my mouth,
 And in my speaking;
God be in my heart,
 And in my thinking;
God be at my end,
 And at my departing.
   The Sarum Primer
   *A Child's Book of Prayers*, p. 13

I see the moon,
 And the moon sees me;
God bless the moon,
 And God bless me.
   Anonymous
   *A Child's Book of Prayers*, p. 14

God make the world so broad and grand,
Filled with blessings from His hand.
He made the sky so high and blue,
And all the little children too.
   Anonymous
   *A Child's Book of Prayers*, pp. 16 and 17

Praise God from whom all blessings flow;
Praise [God], all creatures here below;
Praise [God] above, ye heav'nly host,
Praise Father, Son, and Holy Ghost. Amen.

Day by day, dear Lord, of Thee
Three things I pray:
To see Thee more clearly,
To love Thee more dearly,
To follow Thee more nearly,
Day by Day.

            St. Richard of Chichester
           *A Child's Book of Prayers*, p. 23


Now I lay me down to sleep,
I pray Thee, Lord, Thy child to keep;
Thy love guard me through the night
And wake me with the morning light.

            Traditional
           *A Child's Book of Prayers*, p. 26


O Heavenly Father,
Protect and bless all things that have breath,
Guard them from all evil and let them sleep in peace.

            Albert Schweitzer


**Prayers to be used as Grace Before Meals**

Bless us, O Lord, and these your gifts
which we are about to receive from your goodness.
Through Christ our Lord. Amen.

            *Blessings and Prayers*, p. 20

Thou art great
And Thou art good,
And we thank Thee
For this food.

>              Traditional
>              *A Child's Book of Prayers*, p. 19

For what we are about to receive
May the Lord make us truly thankful. Amen.

>              Anonymous
>              *A Child's Book of Prayers*, p. 7

Be present at our table, Lord;
Be here and everywhere adored.
Thy mercies bless, and grant that we
May feast in fellowship with Thee. Amen.

>              John Wesley
>              *Everyday Prayers for Children*

## One-line Prayers for Children

Thanks be to God.

Glory to God in the highest.

Come, Lord Jesus!

Alleluia!

Lord have mercy.

Stay with us Lord.

May God bless you.

>              *Blessings and Prayers*, pp. 44 and 45

# NOTES

### Introduction

1. Leonard Sweet, *Faithquakes* (Nashville: Abingdon Press, 1994), 160–161.

### Chapter 1

1. Nancy Junge, quoted from an article in *Women in Ministry Newsletter: The Tennessee Conference.* (She serves as Director of Children's Ministries at Bluff Park United Methodist Church in Birmingham, Ala. and is a specialist in worship education for children.)
2. Frederic and Mary Ann Brussat, "Children's Spirituality, A Resource Companion" in *Value and Visions* 24, no. 4 (New York, 1993), 5.
3. Robert Coles, *The Spiritual Life of Children* (Boston: Houghton Mifflin Company, 1990), xvi.
4. Carol Dittberner, "The Pure Wonder of Young Lives," *Sojourners* 16 (January 1987), 21.
5. Marlene Halpin, *Puddles of Knowing: Engaging Children in Our Prayer Heritage* (Dubuque, Iowa: Wm. C. Brown Company Publishers, 1984), ix.

## Chapter 2

1. EvelynUnderhill, *The House of Soul and Concerning the Inner Life* (Minnesota: The Seabury Press, 1929, 1926), 121.
2. Mack B. Stokes, *Talking with God* (Nashville: Abingdon Press, 1989), 13.
3. J. Manning Potts, ed., *The Great Devotional Classics: Selections from the Letters of John Wesley* (Nashville: Upper Room Books, 1952), 10.
4. Saint Augustine quoted in Richard J. Foster, *Prayer: Finding the Heart's True Home* (New York: HarperSanFrancisco, 1992), 1.
5. Richard J. Foster, *Celebration of Discipline* (New York: Harper and Row, Publishers, 1978), 30.
6. Archbishop Anthony Bloom, *Beginning to Pray* (New York: Paulist Press, 1970), 26.
7. C.S. Lewis, *Letters to Malcolm: Chiefly on Prayer* (London: Collins, Fontana Books, 1964), 24.
8. Sofia Cavalletti, *The Religious Potential of the Child*, trans. Patricia M. Coulter and Julie M. Coulter (New York: Paulist Press, 1983), 8–9.
9. Sofia Cavalletti, *The Good Shepherd and the Child* (New York: Don Bosco Multimedia), 13.
10. I am indebted to Bishop Rueben P. Job, retired bishop of The United Methodist Church, for this concept.
11. Rachel Carson, *The Sense of Wonder* (New York: Harper and Row, Publishers, Incorporated, 1956), 45.

## Chapter 3

1. Susanne Johnson, "Christian Spiritual Formation" in *Christian Spiritual Formation in the Church and Classroom* (Nashville: Abingdon, 1989), 103–120. (This book gives a very good account of developmental theories which are rooted in psycho-dynamic thought and in structural-developmental theory.)
2. Mary Ann Spencer Pulaski, *Understanding Piaget: An Introduction to Children's Cognitive Development* (New York: Harper and Row, 1971), 207–208.

3. Brenda Munsey, ed., *Moral Development, Moral Education, and Kohlberg* (Birmingham, Ala.: Religious Education Press, 1980), 91–93.

4. J. Eugene Wright, Jr., *Erikson: Identity and Religion* (New York: The Seabury Press, 1982), 51–54.

5. James W. Fowler, *Stages of Faith: The Psychology of Human Development and the Quest for Meaning* (San Francisco: Harper and Row, 1981), 122–123, 135–136, 151–153, 174–175, 184–186, 199–200.

6. Renzo Vianello, Kalevi Tamminen, and Donald Ratcliff, "The Religious Concepts of Children," in *Handbook of Children's Religious Education*, ed. Donald Ratcliff (Birmingham, Ala.: Religious Education Press, 1992), 58.

7. Ibid.

8. Ibid.

9. Ibid., 61–62.

10. Ibid., 62.

11. Kalevi Tamminen and Donald Ratcliff, "Assessment, Placement, and Evaluation" in *Handbook of Children's Religious Education*, ed. Donald Ratcliff (Birmingham, Ala.: Religious Education Press), 243.

12. Delia Halverson, *How Do Our Children Grow?* (Nashville: Abingdon Press, 1993), 37.

13. Tamminen and Ratcilff, *Handbook of Children's Religious Education*, 244.

14. Henry Van Dyke, "Every Morning Seems to Say," *The Cokesbury Worship Hymnal* (Nashville: Abingdon, Cokesbury Press 1938), No. 291. (From the Children's Year, By Conant. Used by permission of Milton Bradley Co.)

## Chapter 4

1. John H. Westerhoff III, Introduction to the American Edition, Edward Robinson, *The Original Vision: A Study of the Religious Experience of Childhood* (New York: The Seabury Press, 1983), ix.

2. Ibid., 16.

3. Alister Hardy, Preface to Edward Robinson, *The Original Vision: A Study of the Religious Experience of Childhood* (New York: The Seabury Press, 1983), 81.

4.  Westerhoff, *The Original Vision*, xiii.
5.  Neill Q. Hamilton, *Maturing in the Christian Life: A Pastor's Guide* (Philadelphia: The Geneva Press, 1984), 14.
6.  Ibid., 29.
7.  Ibid.
8.  Ibid.

## Chapter 5

1.  Henri J.M. Nouwen, *Life of the Beloved* (New York: Crossroad, 1993), 56–57.
2.  Johanna Klink, *Teaching Children to Pray* (Philadelphia: The Westminster Press, 1974), 9.
3.  Ibid.
4.  Marlene Halpin, *Puddles of Knowing*, 1.
5.  Told by The Reverend David Kerr in a sermon at the Upper Room Chapel while he was on the staff of the General Board of Discipleship, Nashville, Tenn.
6.  Halverson, *How Do Our Children Grow*, 82.
7.  Ibid.

## Chapter 6

1.  Ron DelBene with Mary and Herb Montgomery, *The Breath of Life*, rev. ed. (Nashville: Upper Room Books, 1992).
2.  John Dalrymple quoted in Richard Foster, *Prayer: Finding the Heart's True Home* (San Francisco: HarperSanFranscisco, 1992), 74.
3.  Delia Halverson, *Teaching Prayer in the Classroom* (Nashville: Abingdon Press, 1989), 38–40.
4.  Halpin, *Puddles of Knowing*, 163.

## Chapter 7

1.  One helpful resource is *My Journal: A Place to Write about God and Me* (Nashville: Upper Room Books), for children ages 7–12. Available May 1997. 1-800-792-0433. Order No. UR 791 $14.95.

## Chapter 8

1. Münster Gesangbuch, "Fairest Lord Jesus," *The United Methodist Hymnal*, (Nashville, Tenn.: The United Methodist Publishing House, 1989), No. 189.
2. Mechtild of Magdeburg, *Meditations with Mechtild of Magdeburg*, quoted in DelBene, *The Breath of Life*, 17.
3. This story was related by The Reverend Joyce DeToni Hill at the Academy for Spiritual Formation at Camp Sumatanga, Alabama. She is the pastor of Dimondale United Methodist Church, a suburb of Lansing, Michigan.
4. This story was told by Bishop Kenneth L. Carder at Lake Junaluska, N.C., in July 1996.
5. Sweet, *Faithquakes*, 207.
6. Ronald S. Cole-Turner, "Child of Blessing, Child of Promise," *The United Methodist Hymnal*, (Nashville, Tenn.: The United Methodist Publishing House, 1989), No. 611.
7. Evelyn Underhill, "Light of Christ," by Evelyn Underhill, comp. Roger L. Roberts, *Treasure from the Spiritual Classics* (Wilton, Connecticut: Morehouse-Barlow Co., Inc., 1982), 24–25.

## Chapter 9

1. John H. Westerhoff III, *Bringing up Children in the Christian Faith* (Minneapolis, Minn.: Winston Press, 1980), 49.
2. Frank C. Laubach, *Prayer: The Mightiest Force in the World* (Westwood, N.J.: Fleming H. Revell Company, 1959), 100.
3. Words and music by Christopher B. Hughes, © 1981. Christbearer Music. Used by permission.
4. Laubach, *Prayer: The Mightiest Force in the World*, 85.
5. Merton P. Strommen and A. Irene Strommen, *Five Cries of Parents* San Francisco: Harper and Row, 1985), 72.
6. J. Manning Potts, ed., *The Great Devotional Classics: Selections from the Letters of John Wesley*, 6.
7. I am grateful to The Reverend Danny Morris, Director of Developing Ministries, The Upper Room for this concept.

# SELECTED BIBLIOGRAPHY

Cavalletti, Sofia. *The Religious Potential of the Child*. New York: Paulist Press, 1983.

Coles, Robert. *The Spiritual Life of Children*. Boston: Houghton Mifflin Company, 1991.

DelBene, Ron. *The Breath of Life*. Nashville: The Upper Room, 1992.

Foster, Richard J. *Celebration of Discipline: The Path to Spiritual Growth*. San Francisco: HarperSanFrancisco, 1988.

Foster, Richard J. *Prayer: Finding the Heart's True Home*. San Francisco: HarperSanFransciso, 1992.

Garth, Maureen. *Starbright: Meditations for Children*. San Francisco: HarperSanFrancisco, 1991.

Goodson, Millie S. *The Growing in Faith Library Guidebook for Adults, For Adults Who Love Children Ages 3-7*. Nashville: Graded Press, 1989.

Halverson, Delia. *How Do Our Children Grow?* Nashville: Abingdon Press, 1993.

Halverson, Delia. *Teaching Prayer in the Classroom*. Nashville: Abingdon Press, 1989.

Hamilton, Neill Q. *Maturing in the Christian Life*. Philadelphia: The Geneva Press, 1984.

Hesch, John B. *Prayer and Meditation for Middle School Kids*. Mahwah, NJ: Paulist Press, 1985.

Job, Rueben P. and Norman Shawchuck. *A Guide to Prayer for All God's People*. Nashville: Upper Room Books, 1990.

Johnson, Susanne. *Christian Spiritual Formation in the Church and Classroom*. Nashville: Abingdon Press, 1989.

Killinger, John. *Beginning Prayer*. Nashville: The Upper Room, 1993.

Klink, Johanna. *Teaching Children to Pray*. Philadelphia: The Westminster Press, 1974.

Maberry, Grace W. and L. Barrett Smith. *It's Never Too Early*. Nashville: Discipleship Resources, 1988.

Robinson, Edward. *The Original Vision: A Study of the Religious Experience of Childhood*. New York: The Seabury Press, 1983.

Smith, Judy Gattis. *Developing a Child's Spiritual Growth through Sight, Sound, Taste, Touch, and Smell*. Nashville: Abingdon Press, 1989.

Smith, Judy Gattis. *Teaching Children about Prayer*. Prescott, Ariz: Educational Ministries, Inc., 1988.

Taylor, Joanne. *Innocent Wisdom: Children as Spiritual Guides*. New York: The Pilgrim Press, 1989.

Thompson, Marjorie J. *Family: The Forming Center*. Nashville: Upper Room Books, 1996.

Westerhoff, John H. III. *Bringing up Children in the Christian Faith*. San Francisco: Harper SanFrancisco, 1984.

Westerhoff, John H. III. *Will Our Children Have Faith?* San Francisco: HarperSanFrancisco, 1984.

**Books For Children**

Brown, Margaret Wise. *The Runaway Bunny*. New York: Trophy Picture Book, 1977.

Caswell, Helen. *God Is Always with Me*. Nashville: Abingdon, 1989.

Caswell, Helen. *God's Love Is for Sharing*. Nashville: Abingdon, 1987.

Caswell, Helen. *I Can Talk to God*. Nashville: Abingdon Press, 1989.

Goddard, Carrie Lou. *God, You Are Always With Us*. Nashville: Abingdon Press, 1983.

Gray, Libba Moore. *Miss Tizzy*. Old Tappan, NJ: Simon and Schuster, 1993.

McKissack, Patricia and Fredrick. *When Do You Talk to God?* Minneapolis, MN: Augsburg Fortress, 1986.

Munsch, Robert. *Love You Forever*. Buffalo, NY: Firefly Books, 1994.

**Periodical**

*Pockets*, Jan Knight, editor. Nashville: The Upper Room. Published Monthly (except Jan./Feb.).

**The prayers on pages 154–157 were taken from the following books.**

1. *Blessings and Prayers*. Chicago: Liturgy Training Publications, 1994.
2. *A Child's Book of Prayers*. New York: Henry Holt and Company, 1985.
3. *Prayers for Children*: A Golden Book. New York: Western Publishing Company, Inc., 1974.
4. *Everyday Prayers for Children*. Nashville, Tenn: Dimensions for Living, 1993.

# About the Author

Betty Shannon Cloyd is a diaconal minister in the United Methodist Church and a consultant in prayer and spiritual formation. She was the coordinator of the Upper Room Living Prayer Center from 1993-1994.

The author has served as a missionary in Africa (Zaire), as a home missionary at the Navajo Methodist Mission School in New Mexico, as a director of children's ministries in the United Methodist Church, and as a kindergarten teacher. She holds degrees from Southern Methodist University (B.S. in Education) and Scarritt College (M.A. in Christian Education). She also has studied at Tennesse Technological University and Ecole Coloniale in Brussels, Belgium.

Mrs. Cloyd, author of *Glory Beyond All Comparision* (The Upper Room) is married to the Reverend Dr. Thomas Cloyd. They have four children.